DO399726

Help Desk
100 Success Secrets

Helpdesk

Need to Know topics covering

Help desk jobs, Help desk software, computer

Help desk, Help desk support, Helpdesk jobs, IT

Help desk and Much more

Gerard Blokdijk

Help Desk 100 Success Secrets

Copyright © 2008 by Gerard Blokdijk

All rights reserved. No part of this book may be reproduced or transmitted in any form or by any means without written permission of the author.

Help Desk 100 Success Secrets
- Gerard Blokdijk -

There has never been a Help Desk manual like this.

100 Success Secrets is *not* about the ins and outs of the Help Desk. Instead, it answers the top 100 questions that we are asked and those we come across in forums, our consultancy and education programs. It tells you exactly how to deal with those questions, with tips that have never before been offered in print.

This book is also *not* about a Help Desk's best practice and standards details. Instead it introduces everything you want to know to be successful with and in a Help Desk.

Table of Contents

Which is the Best Technical Support Help Desk Career City in the US? 12

Computer Call Center Help Desk Coping With the Demands of the Call Center Generation 14

Computer Help Desk in a Call Center Environment....................15

Techniques on How to Handle Computer Help Desk Issues......16

What it Takes to be a Computer Operator for the Support Analyst Help Desk...17

Customer Service Help Desk - Pointers to Delivering World Class Customer Service..19

Importance of a Help Desk...21

Another Name for Desk Help Software 22

Entry-Level Helpdesk Computer: The Answer For Small Businesses! 24

Help Desk Computer Operations Officers Working Their Way in Securing Company Premises...26

The Importance of Hiring and Training Help Desk Agents........28

Help Desk Analyst, Not Your Typical Customer Service Agent 30

What You Need To Know About Help Desk Associate and Project Manager Technical Support 31

Top 5 Help Desk Best Practices..33

Help Desk Engineer, A Career Worth Eyeing For 35

Help Desk Jobs, Exciting Yet Challenging 37

Advantages That Help Desk LAN Analysts, PC Technicians Can
Do For Your Business 38

Top Reasons Why You Need To Have Help Desk Management
Software In Your Business 40

Help Desk Managers Making a Difference for Their People 42

Each Level of Support Help Desk Procedures 43

Help Desk Software Applications Tools for Excellent Customer
Service 45

Need for a Help Desk Solution 46

Tips on How to be a Successful Help Desk Specialist 47

The Key Steps in Becoming a Help Desk Support Desktop
Network Engineer 48

Technical and Accounts Services - Most Common Types of Help
Desk Support 50

Help Desk Tech, Billing, Registrations, Retention and
Telemarketing Working Together as a Team 52

The Guide to Being an Expert Help Desk Technical Support
Specialist 53

Help Desk Technician - The Company's Main Man (or Woman)
.... 54

Help Desk Exceeding Customer Expectations 55

Applying Helpdesk Applications 56

Your Guide To Helpdesk Guides 58

Frontline Defense: The Helpdesk Representative 60

The Importance of a Help Desk Call Center 62

How Companies Provide Help Desk Remedies for Stressed-Out
Agents 64

Relieving Help Desks of Help Desk Security Burdens 66

The Benefits of Free Help Desk Support Software 67

Hewlett Packard Help Desk Facility 68

IT Help Desk In-synch with Today's Technology 69

Help Desk Guides to Web Design Computer Programmers 70

An Introduction to the Listening Processes Help Desk Program
....71

Get Access From Your Computer Administrator's Help Desk for
Windows / Unix 73

PC Helpdesk: Computer Desktop Knowledge 101 74

PC Technician Help Desk Does Wonders 76

Relieving Stress for PC Help Desk Support Staff..........................77

Technical Support Help Desk Troubleshooting Internet
Connection Issues 79

The IPR Help Desk - The Help Desk for Intellectual Property
Rights 81

Why Web Help Desk Software is Preferred 83

When to Get Web Help Desk Software Systems for Your Help
Desk 84

Wikipedia Help Desk Knowledge Shared with the World 85

Yahoo Help Desk Features 86

Do I Qualify as a Call Center Help Desk Agent? 88

Requirements to Become a Computer Help Desk Technician.... 90

What is a Computer Operator Help Desk? 92

What Do We Mean By Desktop Help Desk Network LAN Tech

Support PC Tech? 94

Good For Us, We Have Front Desk Help, the Heroic Front

Liners. 96

The Relationship Between Help And Desk And Representative 97

Defining Help Desk Customer Service 99

The Importance of Help Desk Desktop Support........................ 101

Why Work At a Help Desk in New York City?............................ 102

What Does Help Desk Level 1 Status Mean? 104

How Does a Help Desk PC Call Center Handle Angry Callers? 105

Do I Need a Help Desk PC Technician? 107

Treat Your Help Desk Support Specialist As Your First Line of

Defense. 109

Thanks for Help Desk Tech Support 111

The Problem With the Help Desk Telecommute System 113

Hewlett Packard Comes Out With HP Help Desk Services....... 115

What is a Network Help Desk Responsible for? 117

The Indispensable PC Help Desk Support.................................. 119

What Does It Take to Become A Supervisor Analyst Help Desk

Operations Trucking Logistics Officer?...................................... 120

The Finer Points of Web based Help Desk Systems.................. 122

Why IT Organizations Should Invest in Computer Help Desk Software...124

How to Prepare for a Career as a Computer Network Help Desk Technician 126

What Kind of Service Should I Expect From The Dell Help Desk? 128

Understanding What Desktop Help Desk Software Has to Offer Customers..130

Reasons Why Your Business Needs Desktop Support and Help Desk Administration...132

Work of an Entry Level Help Desk Employee............................134

Gain Entry to the IT World Through the Entry-Level in a Junior Level Help Desk Support Position...136

Role of the Help Desk Desktop 3rd Level 137

Help Desk PC Support to Answer Your Needs............................139

Help Desk: How to Troubleshoot With Your Client...................141

Do I Qualify as a Help Desk Administrator? 143

Reasons Why You Need Help Desk Applications in Your Company..145

The Downside of Working as a Help Desk Assistant 147

The Helpdesk Computer is Always on Call..................................149

Solutions for Computer IT Hardware 151

Help Desk Coordinators: What They Can do for You and Your Business...153

Helpdesk: You Are a Specialist in Customer Support...............155

Being a Helpdesk Supervisor 157

What is the Relationship Between the Help Desk, Support Specialist, Technical Support Specialist and Other IT Personnel? 158

The Role of the IT Help Desk Clerk 160

What IT Help Desk Software Covers? 162

Delivering Solutions Through Microsoft Helpdesk Remote Assistance 164

The Work of a Network Administrator WAN Cisco Help Desk Analyst 165

Why Network Administrators and Technical Support Help Desk are Important to Your Company 167

The Basics About the Online Help Desk 169

Help Desk Receptionist: More than Just a Clerical Job 170

Benefits of Software Help Desk 172

The Benefits Derived From Teaching Help Desk Staff 174

Let the Help Desk Support Consultant / Analyst do the Work 175

The Web Based Help Desk Software for you 176

Which is the Best Technical Support Help Desk Career City in the US?

Maybe you are wondering where is the best technical support help desk career city in the United States. The answer is: there is no one place in the US where a career in the technical support help desk department can be said to be the best. Simply because the information technology industry is growing by leaps and bounds everywhere you go. It is possible to get a job in a technical support help desk department in many states throughout the US.

Take New Mexico, for instance. There are different titles for jobs in the technical support help desk departments of many organizations there. Some jobs you may want to look into in that occupation are: IT Specialist, home-based online business systems staffer, Linux System Management Specialist, Systems Development Senior Specialist, and Programmer Analyst, among others. Other states may have other job titles in the same department for which you could be qualified.

To qualify for these technical support help desk careers, you may have to take a mandatory drug test first before being considered for employment. Other requirements can include a complete medical and dental check-up, a background check (particularly if you have worked for other companies, even those not related to the IT industry), proof of citizenship (some employers will not employ aliens, even those nearly finished with their application for citizenship), and security clearance (usually necessary for work with government agencies). Then there is the right background for whichever technical position you are applying for, and perhaps some years of experience in the IT areas you claim to have expertise in. Job experience is a big plus for applicants, because many employers do not want to take a chance on newbies in the business; or if they do give newbies a chance, they will offer generally lower compensation for their services (compared to people with more experience in that IT area.)

Computer Call Center Help Desk Coping With the Demands of the Call Center Generation

Dominate the enterprise. This has been the ultimate goal of a computer call center help desk when talking about the site's performance. Since there are a lot of call centers established in and out of the US, it is a reality that competition is always fierce to meet or exceed the expectations of the client; hence more work (not to mention salary adjustments and bonuses) will be given to deserving help desk agents. Therefore, the performance of the call center is critical in keeping business deals with clients. More satisfied customers means exceeding performance for the site. This also means keeping client value and so, more jobs and perks for help desk agents. More work means job security, so this is something that they should be proud of or even brag about. This is the chain that needs to be in place to keep the business going and moving forward.

So how is the computer call center help desk's performance measured? There are two ways. First is through sending customer surveys. After the interaction, the customer is sent an email containing a list of questions where he or she can grade the help desk agent who assisted them with a computer-related issue. Ranging from poor to excellent, this is where the data for the site performance come from. Another way is through quality checks. There is a team designated to handle monitoring the quality of agent interactions. A specific guideline should be established and make known to help desk agents to maintain the quality of every customer contact. Working together as a team can definitely make call center domination more than achievable.

Computer Help Desk in a Call Center Environment

When you are inside a call center, you cannot help but notice all the emotions surrounding the place. There are some help desk agents who smile before taking a call and rush to the knowledge base tool. While some are okay without any sign of effort, as if they are just taking a normal call. Some are animated, upbeat and lively, while some get a bit frustrated, maybe because the caller finds it difficult to follow the steps necessary to resolve the problem. There are even some who shout for joy when the issue is fixed after a long and very tiring call. This is something that makes a computer help desk agent feel excited, to take another call, since it is indeed very rewarding when you get raving remarks from callers.

The call center is such a very busy place where all the interactions from customers are handled. Usually, the call center is used by mail-order catalog organizations to take product orders from customers, telemarketing companies wherein the agent would call a prospective client and offer him or her products typically at a discounted price, or any large organization that uses the telephone to reach the public when selling different products and services. On the other hand, computer help desks are more active nowadays in the call center industry wherein customer care specialists provide solutions to any computer or product-related issues and concerns. Since new high tech products and computer upgrades are being introduced in the market in just about a smaller span of time, it is definitely a fact that computer help desk call centers are here to stay.

Techniques on How to Handle Computer Help Desk Issues

We all know that computers are prone to software conflicts, hardware malfunctions and security threats (such as virus and spyware infection) that make users go mad. Due to the fact that not everyone in the house is computer savvy, common problems like the ones mentioned may happen. Though almost every household has a computer, not everyone knows how to troubleshoot the usual issues that may be encountered; especially when trying to connect to the internet or to configure programs you've installed. It's because of such cases that computer help desk agents are needed to resolve computer-related concerns, and ensure that the computer stays in good working order.

With computer manufacturers, satisfying customers is a critical aspect of the business. Every interaction is important and it is vital that customer concerns be resolved in a timely manner. Since computer help desk agents are the front-liners of the business, satisfied customers spreading good news through   word of mouth   about the experience they had with customer service is a great marketing strategy. This is an indication of good business, so every interaction counts. Help desk agents need to be made aware of the fact that the assurance of help should be present in every call, to create a positive customer experience. It's normal that once in a while, an irate caller will come to the gateway and complain. When such cases happen, the help desk agent needs to maintain a professional and positive attitude, and leave the member pleased once the call is over.

What it Takes to be a Computer Operator for the Support Analyst Help Desk

First level entry is where the action starts in a support service. It is the level where customers raise their questions and problems either via phone or email. It's also where most customers expect their problems will be taken care of immediately, and preferably right after they hang up.

A computer operator for the support analyst help desk takes care of the diagnostic procedures. The following are some of the duties that such an operator carries out:

1. Answer calls from users that have computer-related problems, or they need assistance in the use of a software application, e.g. a spreadsheet, graphic, database, e-mail or word processing application.
2. Answer questions based on their knowledge of computer operations.
3. Ask questions of the user(s) to assist in diagnosing the problem, find possible solutions and apply the diagnostic procedures.
4. Consult other computer experts to further study the problem and develop solutions, if necessary.
5. Be capable of explaining the errors to the programmers, and recommend changes to the program.
6. Stay abreast of developments, and update their knowledge and skills through continuous communication with computer experts and reading trade magazines, manuals and attend training seminars.

While others may look at first level entry support as not as complex as the other levels, the personnel assigned to this level should be well trained and professionally mannered. They are the organization's front liners in providing service to your customers. A computer operator support analyst help desk does not only require being knowledgeable in computer applications, but they should be trained as well in handling people.

Customer Service Help Desk - Pointers to Delivering World Class Customer Service

What does world-class customer service mean? This term is often heard in call centers, and it may even be included in the company's mission statement. This is the ultimate goal of every call center, to meet or surpass customers' expectations. But, how can this be done? Here are some of the pointers in ensuring that customer service help desk representatives deliver world-class service at all times:

1. Always start the call with an enthusiastic greeting. Thank the customer for calling, as this is an indication that you appreciate them.
2. Remember to make every customer feel that you value them and recognize their importance to the business.
3. Assurance of help should be emphasized at all times. Statements such as: "I can help you with that", will go a long way.
4. Be direct and honest with your responses. If there is a system issue, tell them about it; apologize, but make sure that you mention that it is being worked on.
5. It's okay to be empathetic, but don't overdo it and make the customer feel that it is always the company's fault.
6. Focus on what you can do for the customer. Think of good analogies to make the customer understand the situation better.
7. Be detailed and specific when giving troubleshooting steps. Not all callers are tech savvy. Avoid using technical jargons as much as possible.
8. Give quick responses to every inquiry. Be transparent and put the member on hold, if necessary. Establish

your credibility by sounding confident when giving
resolutions.

Importance of a Help Desk

The information that we have may be limited to a certain degree, and we may require further assistance with problems that we can't handle. It's better to ask rather than assume things, especially if you are dealing with things that you aren't an expert on.

In any organization, there is a place that you can go and ask for assistance and information. In the world of computer technology, the help desk is available to provide information and assistance to users. It seeks to troubleshoot problems related to the computer and its peripherals. Big companies make the help desk support available to their customers via a toll-free number, website and/or email. As you provide help desk to your customers, companies should also provide it to employees.

The typical work at the help desk is to be the focal point person receiving queries, and then provide immediate solutions. A growing company needs to acquire help desk software to efficiently manage all its customers' needs and wants. Help desk software provides an incident tracking system that allows tracking the number of incidents and how they are being addressed, based on the customer's support request. The help desk is the first level of support, and if the issues are solved within this level, the ticket is closed and information is updated as to the solution that was applied to the customer's request.

The real value of the help desk software is recognized to be helpful not only to the customers, but to the organization's computer environment as well. The help desk's capacity to monitor the most common technical problems encountered by users allows the organization to plan for improvements in their products and services.

Another Name for Desk Help Software

Desk Help Software is another (though more unusual) name for Help Desk Support Software. Help Desk Support Software can either be provided through open source access or from copyright-dependent software providers. An open source access product is one that is provided free of charge to end users by the software developer. Their main aim is to make the open source access product widely used, and maybe even become an industry benchmark or standard, as far as help desk support software is concerned.

Whether you call it desk help software or help desk support software, the function of the system is the same: to assist the help desk department, or outsourced the help desk department to help answer the service or product-related queries of end users (meaning anyone from the general public, professionals or otherwise.)

All help desk systems have the commonality of adhering to the following: first, an end user will call in because he has a problem that necessitates seeking customer support from the help desk. Second, the help desk system will present an online help desk form or page for the end user to fill out properly. Then the problem will be assigned to a certain help desk technician who will rank the problem or case according to priority level before he starts searching for resolution. Hopefully, the technician spots the cause of the problem, then comes up with an appropriate solution. After that; the technician will log in the problem and solution, as well as the identity of the concerned end user, into the help desk system; and then present his/her preferred solution to the end user for approval and acceptance.

If your desk help software is a web-based application, it's considered more advantageous, compared to conventional network routed desk help software.

Entry-Level Helpdesk Computer: The Answer For Small Businesses!

Having a helpdesk team is a major advantage in any company. Almost all companies today have helpdesk representatives to attend to the computer and IT product inquiries and problems of customers and clients. But, without the proper helpdesk computer software, the team will surely fail to resolve the customer's problems. There are plenty of entry level helpdesk computer software available for download, to address the needs of small companies.

The primary purpose for establishing a helpdesk is for customers to have support for their computers and other IT related products. Usually, customers will have questions and problems with their product(s) and will want it resolved and answered immediately.

Most companies also have websites for their products. This will usually contain a link for frequently asked questions (FAQ). But, some companies want to save a few dollars, and still answer their clients' questions via email, because they believe that entry level helpdesk computers are an unnecessary expense. However, it's often overlooked that using emails alone is also a time-waster for the helpdesk team because it has no database. Therefore, it's very difficult to track and monitor problems that come in and problems that have been solved. You also can't group together similar problems and solutions when only using email, so your helpdesk team will have to answer each problem individually, even though they have answered it before. Entry-level helpdesk computers have this capability, and can easily cut your helpdesk team's work in half by this feature alone!

Small companies that have entry-level helpdesk computers can easily keep their customers happy and satisfied. They always have updated information on common issues, and can quickly and efficiently resolve them. Remember, even entry-level helpdesk computers have useful and powerful features like customer history, call queue, critical issue alerts, call time management, a knowledge base for FAQ, and many more.

In the end, small companies save more by investing in entry-level helpdesk computers. It will not only keep your customers happy, it will also keep your customers coming back.

Help Desk Computer Operations Officers Working Their Way in Securing Company Premises

One may think that a help desk only supports phone calls from customers who are having problems with the products and services offered by the company. Say for example, a technical support specialist working for a computer manufacturer like Dell Computers gets a phone call about software conflicts or hardware problems. However, there is another aspect of help desk computer operations that happens within the company's vicinity. Here are some of the functions of these help desk officers:

a) Security: It is the help desk personnel's responsibility to make sure that every inch of security is checked and monitored on the computer units set up in the operations department. Installing firewall, antivirus and anti-spyware software applications will definitely prevent external threats like hackers, viruses and malwares from reaching the system.

b) Level 2 Support: Another role of the help desk computer operations officer is to assist co-employees whenever they need help with any computer-related issue or concern. When they have difficulties accessing a certain tool or receive an error message while doing an online job, those are some of the things that help desk officers can provide assistance with.

c) Access rights and network management: When there are newly hired employees, or when somebody transfers from one department to another, it is the duty of the help desk personnel to grant access rights and permissions to these people so that they will be able to use all the tools that they need to perform their jobs. Help desk officers are also assigned to set up computers and tie them up with the company's network.

The Importance of Hiring and Training Help Desk Agents

Companies today concentrate on how to get satisfied and loyal customers. Maintaining a good relationship is the key to keep devoted clients near your tent. Service oriented business should consider help desk as a vital tool in keeping an excellent bond with their clients.

How can help desk agents help your business?

Help desk agents are the front liners of your business. They answer customer queries and vital inquiries. They basically handle assistance requests and update customer data. Help desk agents can make or break the image of your product and company. You have to make sure that they are well trained to deal with furious and intolerant customers. Having these kind of clients are very common to help desks and customer service related businesses. That is why communications with raging clients should be handled with caution.

Agents should also be updated to the latest technology trends and applications. Technology today has a fast growing system that updates regularly. So training on applications is very important to maintain and improve the productively of your company. Every day, systems face unexpected challenges that need solutions fast. One of the challenges is dealing with customers on the phone. You cannot let them wait too long! So help desk agents need to know the system and applications by heart.

The success of satisfying the clients and having them patronize your product and service depend greatly on how help desk agents communicate and answer their queries. Therefore, your company needs to invest in good system applications and excellent training for help desk agents. Being a help desk agent is a tough job. Everyday pressures from the customers and interacting with them personally is not that easy. Agents have to face clients and represent the company appropriately.

Help Desk Analyst, Not Your Typical Customer Service Agent

What are the most effective solutions to a certain problem? What are the frequently asked questions that help desk specialists usually get? How can an agent shorten his or her interaction with a customer on a particular problem? These are some of the questions that a help desk analyst must be able to answer. Basically, the role of the help desk analyst is like a typical help desk agent: answering calls from customer inquiries, opening a ticket for each customer issue, and escalating calls to more experienced agents or Tier 2 support when the problem still persists after all possible solutions have been given. However, help desk analysts have other responsibilities aside from doing the regular stuff. There are the following:

1. Examine and troubleshoot problems using the available tools, such as help desk software, knowledge database and remote control.
2. Manage, maintain and constantly update knowledge base entries.
3. Install and test hardware devices and software applications to study how they react to certain systems and conditions.
4. Respond to any communication, server or network issues.
5. Provide administrative work such as giving network access rights and permissions to specific users.
6. Define and develop inventory procedures.
7. Make sure that help desk agents are up-to-date when it comes to troubleshooting customer issues and requests for training when there is a need for it.
8. Gather relevant data and collect figures taken from the help desk tools to determine the validity of the resolutions given to customers, and track the trouble tickets that need to be escalated.
9. Simplify the process by thinking of better methods on how to get things done.

What You Need To Know About Help Desk Associate and Project Manager Technical Support

Help desk requires competitive people that will ensure the best quality of customer service. Help desk should provide customers the right solutions to their inquiries.

Help desk associates provide assistance to clients that use applications and software. They give solutions to user problems on the phone, and answer the questions and inquires of customers. Answering these queries is the main responsibility of help desk associates. They don't just answer questions, but they also ensure the satisfaction of clients. By communicating professionally to the customers, and giving the right details in a simple and clear manner, help desk associates can satisfy clients in an instant. This unit in help desk team documents and records the calls made by customers and other related functions.

Project manager and technical support.

One of the essential duties of the project manager and technical support is to resolve more complex problems and technical matters. They also track calls and analyze the system change requests. The product manager can define business rules, assess requirements of technology, and configure software applications. Technical support also develops configuration designs and other complex implementations of projects.

Project managers are solution-oriented experts that focus on customer and technical support in the field of communications. They basically specialized in troubleshooting and managing the project requirements. Project managers should be committed to providing great service to the clients. Leadership is also needed; they need to have the people skills to maintain a good relationship with their team. Project managers must initiate goals for the help desk team and make sure their tasks are implemented properly.

Help desk tasks need diverse people to be able to satisfy customers. Help desk associates and project managers / technical support are different units in the IT department, and they help build an organized communication system.

Top 5 Help Desk Best Practices

The help desk is a great customer assistance that you can offer your clients. By simply managing their requests and problems, you can maintain and even increase your clientele. To successfully maintain and support your clients is a plus in giving quality service and value for money.

What is the purpose?

Best help practices are there to equip your IT department, and help desk staff with all the practical techniques you need to maintain excellence in customer service. With the increasing dependence of companies today on technology, implementing IT help desk best practices benefits your company and your clients too.

Here are some points that you want to consider and adopt to improve help desk in your company:

1. Incident management is a process that can reinstate your usual operational service as fast as possible. There are times that technical occurrences take place in your system. This process will minimize the blow to your operations and makes sure that quality is not compromised.
2. Change management can be made if there are factors that affect your system. As much as possible this needs to be done in a controlled manner with less trouble.
3. Creating problem management is one of the best practices for the help desk. In doing so, this process can reduce the amount of difficulties that occur in your department. Without maintaining the right problem management, this could also affect your information system operations.

4. Financial management is equally important. With financial monitoring, your costs can be analyzed and distributed properly.
5. Configuration is an important factor to consider in IT. Managing the configuration is a process that can identify and define the information system that guarantees the accuracy of the system.

These are just five (5) of the best practices that you can adopt in your business. Remember that following these guidelines can better define your costs, increase your productivity and avoid repetitive procedures.

Help Desk Engineer, A Career Worth Eyeing For

One of the most common courses taken by freshmen students in college is engineering. Computer Engineering, Electronics and Communications Engineering, Civil Engineering, Mechanical Engineering, and Marine Engineering are some of the most popular engineering courses available in various universities and technical colleges. Most of these courses have board exams to get a license, which is an essential key to finding a job. However, there are other certifications that one can take to become a certified engineer.

A help desk engineer is one good example. This position is a vital component in the organizational structure of large companies. To become a successful help desk engineer, just go over these steps:

Step 1: Focus on your academic training. To become a help desk engineer, you should finish a Computer Engineering, Computer Science or Information Technology course. It is also a big plus if you have customer service experience in the past, and are proficient with most computer applications.

Step 2: Get your industry-standard certifications such as an A+ certification from the Computer Technology Industry Association, an HDI (Help Desk Institute), and MCDST (Microsoft Certified Desktop Support Technician) certifications.

Step 3: Come in prepared for the interview. Familiarize yourself with the company profile, its staff and partners. Take a closer look at the products and services offered by the company to increase your chances of getting the help desk engineer position.

Step 4: Be creative in answering questions both during the interview and while taking a pre-hiring examination. This will test your thorough understanding of the role of a help desk engineer and its contribution to the company.

Help Desk Jobs, Exciting Yet Challenging

A help desk job is one exciting career, yet challenging at times. It is an exciting profession because if you do it well, it opens a lot of doors for you to take different training opportunities, to travel, and receive excellent perks. Aside from moving up the corporate ladder, you will also be well compensated. You may opt to be promoted to a supervisory position after years of experience, or choose to work as a support team member such as a quality assurance analyst, a trainer or even a network administrator. It all depends on what you want to achieve, and where your heart belongs.

Being a help desk personnel is also challenging at times. First, you have to keep up with the standards set forth by the company, and abide by the quality guidelines to ensure that customers are given full attention and priority. Following a rigorous schedule is another concern for many, where your flexibility will be tested to its limit. There are also times that you might get an irate caller, wherein you need to treat them maturely and confidently. It might also test your patience, but then again, this is all part of the whole package. Staying focused on your objectives and goals will help you in pacifying these kinds of callers.

There are a lot of help desk job postings on the internet. If ever you are interested in applying for one, make sure that you are prepared not only physically and mentally but also emotionally. Loving what you do every day is like you're not working at all. Keeping a proper mindset is the key to call center success.

Advantages That Help Desk LAN Analysts, PC Technicians Can Do For Your Business

Help desk management needs qualified people to help the IT department in your company. Help desk LAN analysts are also PC technicians who systemize your computer and assist your clients and your company.

They are one of the important units in your IT department. They specifically perform the installation and maintain the performance of personal computers and networks in your company. Moreover, user access and network data need to be maintained by LAN analysts.

Other duties and responsibilities:

Help desk LAN analysts are PC technicians who are responsible for resolving problems with any equipment, and operator errors. They troubleshoot application difficulties and track the user's problem request. In any help desk scenario, there are times that clients and company staff encounter technical problems installing and troubleshooting software. Being part of the IT department, the help desk LAN analyst also help in maintaining the company's network access and deleting accounts that are obsolete. In this way, network security is implemented and preserved.

We are all aware that the help desk is a customer related service that helps the clients in any way possible. That is why PC technicians and help desk LAN analysts are responsible to assist the customers in their inquiries and technical problems. Program and system errors are usually a common query that clients ask, especially in IT related businesses. Technicians give support to repair and configure hardware and laptops. That is why LAN analysts and PC technicians should be updated with any changes in computer and IT technology.

IT today is a demanding job that provides great help in maintaining your company's technical support and data networks. With the aid of LAN analysts and PC technicians, you will be able to sustain the quality service that you offer your clients.

Top Reasons Why You Need To Have Help Desk Management Software In Your Business

As we all know, complexity grows everyday in the IT environment. And increasingly, businesses depend on what technology can offer them. It is no longer sufficient to depend on stand-alone help desks. Every day, challenges surface and call for a remedy. Help desk management software is a handy solution for system organization, service level management, workflow patterns, and many more. Your business needs an integrated help desk management that can handle processes and organized services for IT. Help desk management is a convenient way to handle your IT needs. Managing your business or organization can be trouble-free with help desk management software. With the aid of this technology, it automates your help desk system. It includes hardware configurations, tasks, projects and software licenses. Through this tool, you can electronically scan and test your network.

There is help desk software in the market today that provides you with the essential details that you need to know to run your business. This will enable you to remote control your machine. Help desk software makes your system easy to access, and offers you a web interface user-friendly system. It also centralizes your user information, and your software and hardware inventory. Small and medium-sized businesses face the same issues as big companies. The only problem is, small businesses have tight budgets and limited manpower resources. With a limited staff, these businesses need to have a user-friendly system that is easy to apply, yet efficient, and gives customers the satisfaction they need. IT departments review their performance based on their power to help their clients, and provide a smooth delivery and organization to the company. That is why help desk management is very important in coming up with effective software that will support and assist your client inquiries, and organize your corporate system.

Help Desk Managers Making a Difference for Their People

It seems like the presence of the senior leadership in the call center is not felt at all times. Help desk managers are present when there are celebrations, announcements, meetings, and conference calls. It is very seldom that you see them coordinating with supervisors or talking to help desk agents. Does this mean that they are not doing what they are supposed to do? This is a big NO. There is no doubt that the help desk agents are the front liners, giving troubleshooting steps to pacify customer issues and fix their problems. Coaches and team leaders, on the other hand, take supervisory calls and assist agents with almost any call center related concern. But, help desk managers also do their fair share of the game. Though it isn't really felt by everybody, they are working their butts off to insure that everything is under control.

Help desk managers are the ones responsible for keeping track of the issues that agents are constantly dealing with. They summarize these data and formulate a report to determine the effectiveness of knowledge-based entries, and at the same time, give suggestions on how such issues should be addressed. They are also the ones thinking of initiatives to make work easier and more convenient for the agents and supervisors. The ability to relay such significant call center impacting information quickly and accurately to upper management, joined with the efficient supervision of help desk support, are some of the important characteristics of the help desk manager. The overall operation of the help desk is the key indicator on how effective communication and coordination with senior leadership truly makes a difference.

Each Level of Support Help Desk Procedures

Anyone that is seeking help should be heard and attended to. No matter how simple or complex the problem is, as the saying goes: "the customer is always right."

Due to numerous calls and emails received by the support service staff, there developed a need to divide the types of service support that each level provides to the clients. The foregoing paragraphs are what each level of support service consists of:

1. First Level: The personnel assigned does the initial talk to the client. The help desk consultant tries to solve the problem immediately. Consultant must be able to ask basic questions about the PC and its configuration, the error message and the specific event after the problem occurred. If the first level tried to solve the problem, but the client wasn't satisfied with the solutions offered, the first level refers them to the second level.
2. Second Level: The personnel assigned are categorized as specialist. They have technical expertise particularly in troubleshooting support. It also includes technicians that are knowledgeable enough to answer questions about hardware support and networks.
3. Third Level: The personnel assigned at this level handle incidents that are not solved at the second level. A special analysis and programming review of the system applications will be carefully reviewed, and it might take time for the customer to get a reply.

In all levels of support service, the customers are informed and updated through the phone or email. All of the procedures are observed to avoid the piling up of unresolved issues. This procedure is also used to classify the easy, not so easy and difficult issues as they are received and settled.

Help Desk Software Applications Tools for Excellent Customer Service

Multitasking is one of the things that makes help desk support jobs challenging at times. One has to see to it that all the resources provided are maximized in helping customers on every call. While or after talking to the caller, the help desk agent has to leave notes to properly record the reason the customer called to ask for help. These records are used to track the common issues that end-users experience, and thus aid in making adjustments and enhancements to the products or services offered. The tools that customer service representatives use are called help desk software applications. These are must-haves for any help desk operation, to ensure the growth of the business.

Some of the functions of a help desk software program are the following: call management and tracking, trouble ticket administration, account database record keeping and maintenance, and knowledge management. Access rights to these software applications are given to ensure the quality of every interaction. Some of these require a user name and password before access is granted, while some can be accessed using the browser or any desktop application software.

There are a lot of help desk software applications available nowadays; each promises to make it easier for help desk agents to better serve customers during their interactions with them. Some can be downloaded online for free, while some are purchased. Reviews of the programs can be read to help you decide which help desk software application(s) can meet the demands of your business, and the needs of your customers.

Need for a Help Desk Solution

An organization committed to satisfy its customer's needs and wants, will always look for ways to improve its services. Despite all the efforts of seeking solutions to their problems, organizations continue to be bombarded with questions and problems. A company would lose focus on its business activities if inundated with the numerous issues raised by customers. If a situation like that occur, the firm would need to assess its existing operations by hiring a service company that provides help desk solutions.

Help desk solutions started through a comprehensive assessment of the organization's existing operations. Agents and staff are interviewed, and policies and procedures are analyzed. The hardware and technologies are examined, and surveys are conducted to assess customer satisfaction. These findings are written up in a report, and at the end of the assessment a recommendation is to be made to management. Help desk solutions aim to redefine the organization's existing help desk to minimize support expenses and ensure that a high level of customer satisfaction is achieved. Thus resulting in an enhancement of the services provided, and an effective use of the organization's resources.

With the help desk solution, the organization will use the right equipment and/or technology as it fits into the company. The firm can improve the workflow operation by putting the procedures into writing as a standard guide. It will make the help desk work smoother, as there are now standard procedures to observe. The help desk solutions are expected to enhance business operations, fully utilize the organization's staff presence, and ensure that technology within the organization is use at its best fit.

Tips on How to be a Successful Help Desk Specialist

There are lots of departments in a company, each playing a different role geared toward business success. More often than not, each department has its own help desk specialist handling inquiries from visitors, and interacting with co-workers and other business professionals. A help desk specialist should be alert at all times, updating himself or herself with the current events in the department. When a certain report is requested, he or she should know who to talk to, so the work can be done in a snap. Since a help desk specialist is the front liner where questions and concerns from different people are addressed, he or she should be knowledgeable enough to recognize the different issues or concerns surrounding his or her department, and others within the company as well.

A help desk specialist can also answer inquiries and grant requests through the phone or email. He or she calls business associates when a meeting is scheduled to remind them; similar to what an office secretary usually does. He or she can also support technical concerns like computer malfunctions, printer breakdowns and other techie stuff. If not within his or her scope of support, a help desk specialist can also direct the caller to another department to fix their issue(s). A help desk specialist has lots of different functions, but then again, it all boils down to where his or her expertise counts the most. It is indeed a jungle in the corporate world, and recognizing your own potential is very crucial in determining where your passion really is.

The Key Steps in Becoming a Help Desk Support Desktop Network Engineer

The help desk support - desktop network team is a second level support that handles installation of network software, hardware, and maintenance of infrastructure such as switches, servers, firewalls and back-up systems. Network engineers are the backbone of the company's computer infrastructure, since they update the computer network and fix issues when they arise. They are also the ones responsible for network services such as file sharing, email, and security. To be a help desk support desktop network engineer, keep in mind these simple steps:

Step One: Be academically prepared by studying a computer-related course in college. You can take Computer Science, Computer Engineering, Information Technology or any computer / IT degrees.

Step Two: Be a student volunteer. Get a job that handles simple networking setups in your school, like at the library, research center or computer laboratory. If there is no vacant slot available, you can also apply as an intern at various computer-consulting firms.

Step Three: Maximize your available resources. Learn to differentiate the various operating systems, and know how to use them. Read books, and apply what you have learned to be more confident in handling networking issues.

Step Four: Join networking seminars and computer clubs to get updates, and become an expert in the field of networking. Do research occasionally, and share it with the group so the exchange of ideas and information will be free flowing.

Step Five: Work on your communication skills by taking grammar or speech lessons. As a network engineer, you will be interacting with people who are not as tech savvy as you are. Make them realize what you are trying to say by using words that are easy to understand.

Technical and Accounts Services - Most Common Types of Help Desk Support

The call center business is one of the fastest growing industries nowadays. With the great demand for customer service centers to support help desk operations, the hype has stretched beyond the US, reaching the other side of the globe, including countries such as the Philippines, Singapore and India. Help desk support is done mostly through phone call interactions, wherein companies usually allocate a toll free number that customers can use when seeking help. Online support (also referred to as e-support) is also IN at this time. Customers can either send an email or interact with an agent though live chat. E-support is also considered more cost effective than phone support, and is easier to establish and maintain.

Help desk support comes in many different types, the most common is technical support service. Customers or subscribers of various companies (usually IT-based) get in touch with an agent that is part of a team dedicated to answering technical questions, and giving troubleshooting steps to resolve issues. Malfunctioning computers, error messages, the inability to get online, and system issues are some of the common concerns that technical help desk agents get almost every day. Extensive training is also needed to ensure that technical specialists are armed with all technical expertise to better serve customers.

Another type of help desk support is account services. In that, customer service agents get billing and sales inquiries, subscriptions and cancellations, contact information updates, and other account related concerns. Usually, these apply to credit card companies and internet service providers (ISPs). Some agents even entertain both technical and accounts support, depending on the demands of the business.

Help Desk Tech, Billing, Registrations, Retention and Telemarketing Working Together as a Team

A typical call center has a lot of different help desk departments. These could be the following:
(a) help desk tech support handles technical inquiries and resolves computer related issues and concerns;
(b) billing department handles account related inquiries and concerns such as changing of contact and payment information;
(c) registration department takes calls from people who are interested in subscribing to a certain product or service;
(d) retention and cancellation queue where subscribers who would like to cancel are given different options like discounts or a free month service just to keep their accounts; and
(e) telemarketing department, wherein customer service agents are tasked to call potential customers and offer products and services, usually at a discounted price.

Each of these departments plays a major role in giving a different level of customer experience on every interaction. Usually, all these support queues belong to a single client or account. Say, for example, that AOL has all these five departments outsourced to a single call center. The same goes for Dell Computers, Sprint, and Verizon Wireless. The performance of each department is carefully monitored on a regular basis to track what area of concern the client needs to focus on. Training is one option to make the customer service agents aware of the new issues or updates concerning the client's account. If help desk tech is low quality, then revisiting the quality guidelines will definitely help to ensure that world-class customer service is given on every call.

The Guide to Being an Expert Help Desk Technical Support Specialist

When talking about the call center industry, help desk technical support is always mentioned. It is one of the pillars of a strong foundation building toward total customer satisfaction. The quality of every tech interaction needs to ensure that the best possible resolution is given to customers. Here are some of the guidelines that every technical support agent should follow on every interaction:

A) Service with a smile: Greet the customer with all sincerity upon taking their call. Mention your name so that they feel at ease talking to you. Ask for the customer's name to maintain a friendly atmosphere. Practice saying your greeting while wearing a smile on your face and it will definitely make a difference in your interaction.

B) Reassurance of help: Saying the words, "How can I help you today?" is a key indicator that you are willing to listen to the customer's issue. After verifying their concern, say reassuring statements like, "I can help you with your issue," will definitely make the customer feel that he or she made the right choice in calling technical support.

C) Active Listening: Listen carefully, and write down the different keywords that the customer utters, so you better understand the problem.

D) Maximize resources: Use your tools efficiently. Give the best possible resolution on every interaction.

E) Closing remarks: Before ending the call, ask if they have any other issue(s) that they need addressed. Thank them for calling and tell them to call you back for further assistance.

Help Desk Technician - The Company's Main Man (or Woman)

When there is something strange happening in your computer, who are you going to call, the ghostbusters? Nope, the help desk technician can definitely save the day. People seek the advice of help desk technicians when they need assistance with their computer, any hardware device or software application. As a requirement, these professionals need to listen diligently to the problem being described, ask probing questions (when necessary) to isolate the issue, and take methodical steps to analyze and solve the problem. It is also important to always be ready to switch lanes when new facts become available during the course of the interaction.

Usually, a help desk technician is seen as being at the front of every battle, resolving customer issues, while armed with true passion for work and great knowledge obtained from books and experience. On the other hand, there are also help desk technicians that work at the backend, maintaining the network of large companies and serving co-employees when they encounter computer problems.

Aside from having good communication and listening skills, it is also important that a help desk technician possess excellent writing skills. When assisting a caller, either a customer or co-worker, the help desk technician has to document the interaction and write down essential points to track which solution resolved the issue. This not only enhances their knowledge database, but also, writing notes will help the next technician who assists the same caller, if they call again. The technician can determine the next possible step, if every solution given previously failed to fix the problem. Truly, being a help desk technician is not easy, but it is justly rewarding at the same time.

Help Desk Exceeding Customer Expectations

"You have reached (Company/Product Name) customer support. My name is (Agent Name). How may I help you today?" This is a typical opening statement a caller would hear when asking for support from a customer help desk specialist. Assurance of help is always emphasized, as these support systems are designed to be of service to the end user of a certain company or product. Help desk support agents are considered the firm's front liners; making sure that customer value is maintained to the standards set forth by the company. Customer help desk service is a very crucial aspect toward reaching company success.

When someone applies as a help desk agent, the very first quality that the interviewers look for is good communication skills. Since the work is more interacting with customers and dealing with their concerns, a person who can effortlessly express his or her thoughts through words that can be easily understood by the caller is definitely an advantage. Meeting customer needs is a top priority, so being armed with excellent communication and customer service skills are the ingredients in making sure that the promise of providing high quality service is something that customers can expect on each and every call.

Nowadays, other companies are also offering live chat and email support to their customers, aside from posting answers to frequently asked questions (FAQs) on their web site. Information or steps to perform are usually stored and maintained on a database that the agent can access when providing resolutions. Truly, help desk support has gone way beyond customer expectations.

Applying Helpdesk Applications

Companies today are ever expanding their business undertakings. To keep and maintain happy and satisfied customers, helpdesks have become a standard in any organization - even schools have helpdesks! In this line, a good helpdesk software application is a must, in order for the company to properly manage their data, contact information and references.

Technologies are advancing to levels that were only imagined a few years back. With so many advanced products and services, many customers are getting confused and finding it hard to keep up with the IT innovations. Most of them know that they need the product or service, but have little or no idea on how to go about maximizing it. In order to address these needs, helpdesks have been established not just for the organization's customers, but for its business partners and clients as well.

In order for a company to completely address the needs of their customers, they must also have good helpdesk software applications. They cannot just establish a helpdesk, hire people and pray to the heavens that everything will run smoothly. An organization will also need to invest in a good helpdesk application in order for them to address the needs of their clients and customers. This helpdesk application should enable the company to maximize their helpdesk representatives, and create a system that is effective, efficient, organized and updated. Whether it is an email, telephone or internet based inquiry, the helpdesk application should be able to handle all incoming and outgoing transactions with no loss of quality.

If you are looking for helpdesk applications, there are many out there ready for download. They can be free (for simple uses) or with a fee (for advanced users and big companies). Or, if you want, you can even have a customized helpdesk application built for your company. Make sure that it's easy to use and is able to track everything from incoming/outgoing calls to the speed of transactions.

Investing in a good helpdesk application will not only make you more efficient in handling customer and client support, it will also help you keep them happy and satisfied.

Your Guide To Helpdesk Guides

Helpdesks are an important part in any organization. Research has shown that it is costlier to find new customers than keep the old ones. So, it is imperative that a helpdesks be set up in every organization to maintain an excellent customer relationship. A simple and easy to follow helpdesk guide for customers to effortlessly identify and resolve their problems is the dream of all establishments.

A helpdesk is an information and resource database that assists, guides, troubleshoots and offers solutions to computer problems and other IT related products. Usually, it is accessed via the phone, email or the internet. It can either have a team of customer service representatives or have a link to frequently asked questions (FAQ).

In establishing a helpdesk guide, companies should keep records of all helpdesk transactions and analyze them properly so that similar problems are grouped together for easy reference. Since most companies have websites that contain a link to FAQ, grouping similar problems and creating a simple summary of solutions can be an advantage to the company. Helpdesk guides should not be confusing and troublesome for customers and clients, especially if they are not very familiar with the product. We should always remember that the first level of resolving problems or questions usually starts with the FAQ; so your helpdesk guide should be concise, clear, and easy to follow to avoid dissatisfied customers. Having a team of helpdesk representatives will also be beneficial to your company in the event that the helpdesk guide cannot solve or answer the inquiries of the customer. The main purpose of the helpdesk representative will be to directly interact with and handle the customer's questions efficiently.

Keeping customers happy is one of the most important objectives of any company. Having an excellent helpdesk guide to immediately resolve any inquiries is the first step to keeping the customers happy and keeping them loyal to your company.

Frontline Defense: The Helpdesk Representative

Many companies are expanding their business and are focusing more and more on customer satisfaction. In order to maintain a good customer relationship, companies now have helpdesks to address or assist customer needs and inquiries. A staff of good help desk representatives can make the difference between a satisfied and unsatisfied customer.

The helpdesk representative is responsible for the proper handling of customer inquiries, and requests for assistance. He will be responsible for the creation and updating of customer data, so that future lookup, retrieval and cross-referencing will always be in order. The helpdesk representative should always be up to date with the latest trends, procedures and processes of his job. Attending training sessions, seminars and workshops related to his job is recommended.

Becoming a helpdesk representative is not an easy job. It requires the employee to directly and personally interact with the customer on behalf of the company that he works for. This means that the helpdesk representative should have extensive knowledge of the company profile, policies and procedures, including its history, in order to properly address a customer's needs. He is the frontline person of the company.

Customers are becoming more and more demanding, and the idea that they do not have to buy from a company, or avail themslves of the firm's services has put most companies on the defensive. Finding new customers is a hard job. Keeping them is even harder. That is why the helpdesk representative should always be available for whatever needs the customer may have for the product or service that he purchased.

But, helpdesk representatives need not be confined to customer service alone. Business partners and clients also need to be properly handled, and most of the time, helpdesk representatives are the first persons they will encounter if they have any inquiries, updates and/or proposals.

The helpdesk representative: truly, the company's frontline person for complete customer and client satisfaction.

The Importance of a Help Desk Call Center

When you think of a Help Desk Call Center, you usually think of the benefits these help desk systems provide to end users like yourself. People who belong to the general public, who may or may not have information technology skills, but they may possess the commonality of needing support from the help desk in IT-related problems. However, there is another entity that benefits from the existence of the help desk call center, and that would be the organization being served by the help desk call center.

A help desk call center can exist in two ways: either the organization it serves runs it, or it outsources that function to a separate private company that specializes in help desk call center services. Organizations may choose to outsource because it relieves their staff of the stress of providing that function themselves. At the same time, the organization benefits because the help desk call center services service provider may have more flexibility in operating such technical support services. The mother organization then gains more time, resources, and manpower to devote to its core concerns.

Organizations that have many users who belong to different user-type categories, or who may have many branches, offices and networks in different geographical locations, may find it ideal to outsource their help desk call center function to professional service provider companies. When looking for the right service provider, the decision-makers for the organization should try to identify the type of infrastructure the service provider uses for its help desk system, its operational experience in providing resolution to customer-related problems, and its scope of management expertise. To sum up, an ideal help desk call center services service provider must have enough technology, processes and people to do the job the way it should be done.

How Companies Provide Help Desk Remedies for Stressed-Out Agents

Day in and day out, call center agents (also known as help desk professionals) are placed front and center in a grueling work environment, and then beset by grumpy, rude, unprofessional and sarcastic callers. At the same time, these help desk professionals have to contend with long work hours, and having to rush to fill their daily quota. On top of this, they have to follow every necessary company standard when it comes to operations protocol, just to keep their job and be paid regularly. This is why help desk remedy becomes important for stressed-out agents.

Getting a job with a help desk company may be the easy part. It is keeping it as a regular day job (or night job - if you factor in mandatory graveyard shifts and compulsory flexible working hours) that gives help desk professionals a headache.

What is it exactly that makes a caller become as rude as they can when the help desk staff answer their call? Even agents are tempted to ask the caller about this sometimes. Can the caller possibly get even ruder; agents are probably just aching to ask.

Well, callers are often rude because of the product-related or service-related problem they're facing. It makes them feel frazzled and hassled. In turn, agents may react in an offensive manner to the caller because they too are stressed every day while at work. You can rarely find callers on certain days who maintain a positive attitude. On those days, they voice their grudges full steam into the ears of the poor helpless agent.

With all the stress that agents have to contend with, companies usually compensate them well for the pressure of being help desk assistants by offering nice, even generous benefits. Usually, in a big call center company, you will find good facilities that are maintained just for their agents - like a video arcade, resting place, and even a gym. Such companies pamper their employees with great health benefits, insurance, dental care, and of course the mandatory high salaries. Their regular employees enjoy paid leaves or vacation time as well.

Though all these are nice benefits for a person who works as a help desk staffer, it is still a basic necessity to provide adequate training to them. That way, they can keep improving on their level of knowledge and skills, so that most (if not all) calls have a successful conclusion.

Relieving Help Desks of Help Desk Security Burdens

When we speak of help desk security, we usually refer to the authentication technique used by help desks. It consists of asking the user to provide a valid username and registered password, before they can avail themselves of the help desk function. For this technique to be applicable in real situations, it is necessary that users take responsibility for providing complex, undecipherable passwords for their username file, and then keep updating them so that they remain undecipherable to intruders or identity thieves. But, in practice, passwords get forgotten, jumbled in the mind of the user, and may eventually expire. When this is the situation, the help desk system gets stressed because its IT personnel have to help these users out of their jam. These IT personnel thus waste valuable time, resources, skills and energies in assisting users, when the IT staff could be applying themselves to other important IT-related projects for the organization.

One solution to this common trend is for IT help desk managers to provide a self-service security protocol to the help desk system. In this way, users are dependent on their own intellectual capabilities at managing passwords (even when they tend to mix them up from different systems, or completely forgot them.) At the same time, the security protocol of the help desk is not jeopardized, since strict security policies are still adhered to by the help desk staff and followed by the users.

All users need to be granted access somehow to the help desk network, because this is where they get to use various resources. Some common resources that end users can easily avail themselves of, when a self-service security protocol is in place, are portals, online services, websites, data, and applications.

The Benefits of Free Help Desk Support Software

Help Desk Support Software is the program used by different organizations for their respective help desk departments and systems. You probably think help desk support software is quite expensive to invest in, right? Actually, that is true. Fortunately, for those who would prefer to keep their money for other needs, they have the option of getting free help desk support software instead.

No need for raised eyebrows, there really are software developers who create help desk support software, then give it away to the general public through downloads from their website. One type of free help desk support software is based on the PHP codes, and it can easily be downloaded and installed in your hardware through a help desk installation wizard. It relies on the free MySQL database program, it doesn't need much database or programming knowledge from the person installing it, or the end users, and it can be updated using the versions released periodically by the manufacturer (the software developer).

There are some other things that you should look for in free help desk support software. It helps if the software developer has a feedback mechanism where they actively solicit suggestions, comments, and ideas that can help them make future versions better. Some might even host a software discussion forum where you can interact with other users of the software (and its different versions), so you can get tips on how to further integrate and apply that help desk support software into your organizational processes. These two features allow pre-existing bugs in the different versions of the software to be reported to the software developer, so they can churn out more effective and efficient versions in the future.

Hewlett Packard Help Desk Facility

Hewlett Packard is a company that caters to providing hardware and software products for home and home office, small and medium businesses, large enterprises, government, health and education. Hewlett Packard covers even supplies and accessories. As a result, the growing numbers of customers demand more attention, and when problems arise, an immediate solution should be made available. Due to the various products that it offers, the HP experts are always available to answer queries, may they be simple or complex, on a 24/7 service. To keep its customers updated and to track customers' inquiries/problems, the company created the HP Total Care Facility to address the needs of its buying public. The following are the benefits that it provides:

1. The HP website is available 24/7 and is loaded with diagnostic tools, software updates, security tips and troubleshooting hints.
2. Free online classes on " Tune Up your PC" and "Getting Started with Digital Photography."
3. Get access to HP's knowledgeable technicians that will answer questions on "how to" handle a problem with the product that is not covered by a warranty.

The HP help desk also provides a search engine to direct customers to a specific product, and it allows customers to download drivers, once they've given the system the product's code. There are links to inform users of the nearest service support, should a technician need to see the product. There are also options provided for customers to choose how to get in contact with HP.

The HP help desk greatly helps it to continuously provide good quality products and services, thus earning big profits as well.

IT Help Desk In-synch with Today's Technology

Have you recently signed up for a broadband connection, but then suddenly it is no longer working for some unknown reasons? Are you sick and tired of having to restart the computer over and over again, when the screen freezes while you are accessing a web page or a certain software application? How does it make you feel when you are about to reach the end of an online game and all of a sudden, you received an error message that says: "This program has performed an illegal operation." It's pretty annoying and devastating, isn't it? When you encounter such cases, you can't help but think that there is something wrong with your computer system. The IT help desk will definitely help you in this regard. All you have to do is sit back, relax and call an IT help desk agent.

IT help desk is a growing industry, since more and more IT-related products and services are being sold to the public. Computers, internet-enabled cellular phones, and music gadgets like ipods are just some of the innovations that people use in his everyday life. Each of these products has a specific department called IT help desk, where customers can call to report an issue or problem. Do not considered them to be your regular day-to-day friendly neighborhood customer service agent. IT help desk agents' job is a little more complicated and sensitive; so being armed with the right tools and knowledge will make a challenging task easier.

Help Desk Guides to Web Design Computer Programmers

Your company's website is your storefront on the internet. Consumers these days go first to the internet and try to look over the information about goods or services, prior to buying or at least trying it. First impressions most often prevail in our choice of things. Make your product appealing to the viewers, so they will keep on viewing your website, and learn more about your company and products.

The IT web design computer programming help desk seeks to help companies come up with a website design that can be easily understood by viewers. Thus they can get an overview of the company and its products and/or services. There are also books available for IT web design computer programmers that provide detailed instructions and specific help on the task at hand. The help should include topics on the actions that learners must undertake when faced with problems on the program. The topics within the help facility should be co-related, and not mixed up with irrelevant sub-topics. It would be best if the web design help desk could provide a glossary of the reference terms used with the terminologies of the web site design. Clickable icons should be made available for easy links on the topics that viewers would like to look at. A search engine bar for viewers to type into should be available to gain information on the item to be viewed. It may also be necessary for an advanced search feature to be present.

The IT web design computer programming help desk is a tool to aid programmers in creating website designs for companies. The website being the virtual store, should always be updated in order to maintain a cutting edge in the marketplace.

An Introduction to the Listening Processes Help Desk Program

The ability to listen is one of the most important skills a help desk agent should have. Without this skill, a call cannot be pursued to its best conclusion, because a perfect two-way communication process will never be achieved if one has poor listening skills. That is why a help desk or call center company usually provides training for listening comprehension. It is a must that a help desk agent be equipped with good listening skills.

Call center listening training process.

There are two types of exams that offer training in listening. These are help desk basic spelling and help desk advance spelling. Audio recordings are provided to the agent, who is required to listen and correctly spell the words spoken. (Most of the words are the ones agents most commonly misspell.) The difference between these two listening exams is that the basic program requires the agent to type or write the words correctly, while the advanced program asks the agent to just spell the words correctly.

Another type of listening program is the call center simulation system. This is where a help desk administrator mimics callers by talking directly through headphones (trying to be as real as a help desk call can get), while the test taker (or agent) must respond correctly (according to pre-set standards of the company). After the simulation is over, printed comments and suggestions on how he can improve his performance are given to the test taker, so he can bone up on his weak points.

Help desk data entry is another audio training program provided. Here, a database of audio recordings is provided. The agent is required to type in information from the audio file correctly. It measures listening skills, as well as precision in typing.

The help desk environmental exam is a test where an agent is required to listen to an audio file. It's provided by the help desk administrators, to test an agent's speed and accuracy in typing orders, receiving questions, and solving them with absolute capability.

Get Access From Your Computer Administrator's Help Desk for Windows / Unix

Putting the right technology in your organization involves a lot of monetary investment. The maintenance and administration of computers also covers a large of portion of the company's budget. But, it surely pays off when you know that products and services are delivered to customers when they need them.

Being in a computerized organization, where various software applications are available for the operations of your business, there is a need for someone who will administer the operations of the company's server. A focal person should be available 'round the clock to ensure that hardware and software are running smoothly, and full monitoring of the network operations are carried out. As an operator administrator help desk for windows and Unix, expertise on the operations is required. He has the power to grant access to users, as well as have a full view access of the operations within the organization's computer environment.

Inasmuch as the support service's first level requires ticket tracking; the operator administrator help desk for Windows / Unix should be able to track down records of customers' requests, and be able to determine which among these requests were acted upon by departments within the organization. It should also allow them to make a report to management as to which support requests are not being acted upon, either due to a complex situation or to the problem being set aside for a reason. Windows / Unix servers have a feature that can identify the desk agent that handles their request.

PC Helpdesk: Computer Desktop Knowledge 101

Investing in a desktop computer can be a difficult problem, especially if you are not very familiar with the IT industry. This PC helpdesk for computer desktop will try to help you by giving you a few pointers on how to choose the best PC. There are two kinds of desktop computers, the PC and the Mac. Since we are primarily focusing our helpdesk on the PC desktop, we will not discuss the Mac.

With new computers becoming more and more powerful, novice PC users find it difficult to identify which computers have the right power for them. This PC helpdesk for computer desktops is your answer.

In looking for a PC desktop, the following should be considered: budget, function and power. You have to know your budget in looking for a desktop computer, and you have to stick to it as much as possible. Entry-level computers will usually range in price from $200 to $400. High-end computers will be much higher.

Ask yourself this question: For what purpose will I use my computer? PC helpdesks are often flooded with questions on computer use because most buyers have no idea what the purpose of their computer is. Buying a high-end computer desktop for simple word processing is not a good idea. Many desktop PCs nowadays are powerful enough to meet your needs, so if you're not going to use it for heavy graphics and video editing, it would be wiser to invest in an entry-level computer desktop.

You want to go techie? Then you should understand that your PCs power is very important. Therefore, for light computing, the minimum requirements for today are dual-core processors.

Intel is still the most popular brand (and it shows with their share of the market). Memory should at least be 512MB and a Hard Disc of 80GB. With prices of PC desktops falling almost daily, you can probably get a better deal at lower prices, yet with higher specifications.

So there it is. You're now ready to face the IT world with this PC helpdesk on computer desktop.

PC Technician Help Desk Does Wonders

Maintenance of computers covers a big share of your company's budget. As your computer bogs down, you wait for a technician to have a look at it. But, it may take days or weeks before your technician pays you a visit. Your productivity is affected, and you are unable to meet your targets.

A solution to the wait time for your technician is software that allows a nationwide remote access of what your computer needs i.e. services, repair or support. With the PC technician help desk software, support service friendly technicians have the ability to connect to your computer via high speed Internet, and troubleshoot and find solutions to your PC's problem. It is a remote control system that automatically connects your PC to your technician. The PC technician can fix your PC without having to sit next to you. The technician can log in/out, reboot or log in using safe mode, even when the user is away from the keyboard. PC technician help desk software seeks to help solve the following:

1. Slow Computer Activity.
2. Unexplained / Excessive Pop-ups.
3. Unexplained Browser Changes.
4. Email Configuration.
5. Virus Removal.
6. Spyware Removal.
7. Wireless Network Security Issues.
8. Basic Wireless Network Connection Issues.

The PC technician help desk is economical, and delivers services immediately. You don't need to go on leave from work or stop your regular duties to attend to a visiting technicians at your home or work just to have your PC fixed. Your PC is fixed via remote control.

Relieving Stress for PC Help Desk Support Staff

Why is PC help desk support so important to the public nowadays? Well, in these times, nearly everyone is immersed in interactions with computers all the time. This ranges from students, to professionals at work, and can even include people who run home-based businesses. Computers have become a necessary part of our everyday lives. So, you should not wonder why PC problems arise every day, and why the PC help desk support system is so important to the general public.

The objective of being a PC help desk support staffer is to help your callers from going out of their minds due to unsolved PC problems. You need to possess significant computer literacy, and other information technology skills, to be successful if you pursue this career path. However, it is not only your knowledge that you depend on to reap the valuable fruits of working as a PC help desk support agent. You will need to possess and maintain a mental and psychological balance, if you want to continue with your job and reduce your stress levels.

Unlike other jobs where one foul-mouthed statement from the other party will land that person with an oral defamation lawsuit quicker than a slap in the face, the PC help desk support agent is forced to deal with the fact that almost all callers are having a bad day. It is the job of the agent to rely on his skills for the benefit of the callers, even if the callers are annoying or obnoxious.

How can the public make the job of a PC help desk support agent much easier for him or her to bear? For one thing, if you call, be as nice as the agent that answers your call. If the agent greets you with a cheerful "Good Morning," then answer likewise. If the agent is accommodating, be just as gracious in your replies. If the agent is respectful, do not forget your own manners. Granted, you are facing a tough problem, but the agent will help you. There is no need for expletives, raised voices, or sarcasm.

Technical Support Help Desk Troubleshooting Internet Connection Issues

Currently, the most common types of connections that customers use to link with the internet are dial-up and broadband. When customers are having difficulties connecting to the internet and accessing websites, they usually turn to the technical support help desk to have their concerns addressed and resolved as fast as possible.

If a customer is on a dial-up connection, what are the possible reasons why he or she is unable to connect to the internet? Here are some of them:

(1) Phone line issues: It could be that the phone that the customer is using does not have a dial tone. It is also possible that line noise or interference prevents the modem from dialing up. Another possibility is that a bad weather conditions like heavy winds, thunderstorms or typhoons are causing a very bad phone line.

(2) Incorrect physical connections: Make sure that one end of the phone cord is connected to the wall and the other end is connected to the computer's modem on the port that says Line or Telco.

(3) Outdated modem settings: The modem may not be functioning as designed, causing the customer's inability to connect to the internet. The modem should have an updated driver to make sure it is in good working condition.

(4) Bad Access Numbers: Heavily congested access numbers may cause the problem. Report the issue as soon as possible and have the customer dial a different number.

If the customer is connecting via broadband, here are some reasons for poor connectivity:

(1) System Maintenance: Check for current system maintenance in the customer's area.

(2) Unstable broadband connection: If the customer is unable to access the internet using the browser, then help him or her in reconfiguring the connection.

The IPR Help Desk - The Help Desk for Intellectual Property Rights

In the European Union, questions regarding the laws on Intellectual Property Rights (IPR) in member countries can be referred to the IPR Help Desk. It operates under a mandate from the European Commission. It aims to function as the first line of support for EU-RTD contractors who have, and may eventually secure, business dealing in some way with Intellectual Property Rights.

The IPR Help Desk does not charge people when they make inquiries. It is a service that has the backing of a partnership consortium based in Spain, Germany and Poland.

The other functions of the IPR Help Desk are:
(1) make the general public aware of the vital need to safeguard IPR assets within European jurisdiction;
(2) allow the use of those critical IPR assets when needed (particularly if the IRP-related projects are based on research and development of the FP6 category, has funding from the European Union, and/or are covered by the European Commission European Research Area Initiatives);
(3) support European research groups or individual researchers when they pursue Intellectual Property projects;
(4) entertain candidates for future research programs that may eventually receive funding from the European Union; and
(5) generally grant the necessary knowledge about registration, protection and proper usage of Intellectual Property Rights to the affected European researchers.

The IPR Help Desk maintains a site at www.ipr-helpdesk.org that people using different languages can readily access. The IPR Help Desk can also be reached through its email address at ipr-helpdesk@ua.es.

However, the IRP Help Desk does have its limitations. It cannot supply inquiries about legally binding stipulations in IPR. It only aims to heighten awareness about the need to know how, why and when IPR affects researchers in the European Union.

Why Web Help Desk Software is Preferred

Providing technical and customer support assistance may not be the core mission of a business, however it is their mission that customers be satisfied. A dissatisfied customer is a great loss to a business. When computer systems at work becomes a problem, it is most likely that it will affect the productivity or performance of the business as the company fails to deliver their product/services. Worst of it all, customers may go and find another firm that provides better service. For a growing company, customer support is a necessity. You need to be aware of what your customer needs and wants are, and seeks solutions should there be problems that require actions.

Make things easier for you and your customers. Make your customers happy and find solutions to satisfy them. Outsource a support service, or have your own support people at work come up with a tool that customers can access from the company's website to address their concerns. Use a web help desk software to allow management to track down records of complaints and how actions have been undertaken. This will enable management to monitor staff/departments as to their performance. Employees' performance is monitored and the various problems that they receive from customers are evaluated. From this information, you'll be able to come up with decisions on your next step toward enhancement of your products and services. The web help desk software allows customers to interface with the company, and also allows them to track their request status.

The Web help desk software is a tool to allow customer support to handle things easier. It allows you to continue to attain your objective of earning profits, and at the same time provide good quality of service.

When to Get Web Help Desk Software Systems for Your Help Desk

If you find the help desk for your organization to be swamped because of the volume of requests it handles and the number of departments in your organization that it has to serve, then perhaps you may consider securing web help desk software for your help desk system.

The web help desk software solution you procure needs to have certain features to make it an effective and efficient solution. It should, of course, be web based; use different back-end databases; and have PC and Mac compatibility. There are web help desk software solutions that are founded on the Java system and adhere to industry standards for web help desk software products. This means the preferred solution will possess database and platform independence; inherent clustering support for its scalability features; yet maintain a user interface that is simple to use, attractive, and perhaps even intuitive. The platforms that your preferred solution relies on could be: Solaris 8, Linux, Windows Server, and Mac OS X.

It also helps if you look into the background of the people and organization that supply the preferred web help desk software solution you are considering. If the software development company has a reputable team of web application developers who are focused on enterprise web applications (such as the previously-mentioned Java system), then that is one point in their favor. You should also ask them for a list of satisfied customers who have used the product before. Then you can ask those customers how effectively and efficiently the product performed for them.

Wikipedia Help Desk Knowledge Shared with the World

Wikipedia is one of the most frequently visited sites on the internet today. It provides answers to almost any question that you can think of, be it in the field of science and technology, mathematics, entertainment, politics and the arts. It is like a main library of facts, figures and fiction that can satisfy any curious mind. If there is a topic or subject that readers want to be posted on the site, all they have to do is post it by clicking the link provided on the Wikipedia Help Desk site, and a group of volunteers will help in finding an answer. Wikipedia is still in the process of development, and feedback coming from its users will definitely aid in making it the primary source of information on the World Wide Web.

To reach the Wikipedia Help Desk page, just type in the words "Wikipedia help desk" in the Search field on the main page of Wikipedia, and results will be generated in a flash. Click on the Wikipedia Help Desk link, and you'll be taken to its help desk site. The Wikipedia Reference Desk, on the other hand, functions like the Wikipedia Help Desk. It acts like a library reference desk, wherein it helps users go to the topic that they wish to locate. Before a request is made to feature a topic or subject that users want to be posted on Wikipedia, the reference site encourages them to type in the topic on the Search first, or click on a specific category where the subject most likely belongs. The help site is indeed user-friendly and easy-to-use; it could be even better than talking to a live person.

Yahoo Help Desk Features

Everyone nowadays uses computers. Even kids at school are taught how to use computers and search the internet. Everyone knows the popular website Yahoo. Yahoo provides a wide variety of internet services that cater to almost any kind of online activities. It is for that reason that yahoo has become one of the favorite website search engines.

Since help desk provides information and assistance, the Yahoo help desk ensures that each Yahoo directory has a help facility. Unlike other help desks, Yahoo help desk does not provide the Yahoo phone number, but an email address instead. It has features like providing topics for frequently asked questions, suggestions, and trouble-shooting procedures, all made available to help users if problems should arise. Other than each directory having its own help facility, it has a Yahoo Central website that lists all the Yahoo services and help facility information. Related helpful links are also provided, and they include:

1. Help in Signing in and Registration.
2. Help in Marketing Preferences. This has to do with the option of whether you want to receive advertisements from marketers over the internet.
3. How to report an abuse. This has to do with scams and spams your account receives.
4. Help in securing your Yahoo account.
5. Security Center. This has to do with protecting your PC from viruses.
6. Private Policy. This has to do with keeping personal information of users private.
7. How to make Yahoo your home page.

Yahoo desk help not only serves the needs of the users, but itself as well. They made the Yahoo desk help solutions ready, and designed them for easy user access.

Do I Qualify as a Call Center Help Desk Agent?

The staff of a call center help desk is made up of a group of very technically skilled people, whose duty is to help callers stuck with service or product-related problems. The call center help desk is considered a type of support group formed by a company to manage problems related to their products and/or services. Callers help provide much-needed user-based information to the help desk, which also handles inquiries.

You must meet certain qualifications, if you apply to become a call center help desk agent. One of them is the willingness to work with flexible schedules, such as assuming the graveyard shift and working during holidays. Your potential salary should match your level of experience and training. All calls you receive must be dealt with as a professional, which means you need to be friendly, observe good manners, and adhere to high standards for customer satisfaction.

It is essential that a call center help desk agent be responsible for securing accurate identification of the callers. They are also required to reach their quotas, a specified number of calls to be reached, at the end of their shifts, and follow company procedures and policies. With a given talk-time, agents must follow regulations on how long or how short the call should be, so that problems are identified and solved within that timeframe.

Good communication skills, technical knowledge about computers, honesty, dependability, and good touch-typing skills are always a plus when you are aiming for a career in a call center.

If you are hired, you can expect benefits like health insurance, dental insurance and perhaps even life insurance to be offered by your employer. Paid sick leave, and vacation leaves are also offered, provided you meet the standards for agent performance. Considering that you exist in a working environment that focuses on helping people, being a call center help desk agent is a very admirable profession.

Requirements to Become a Computer Help Desk Technician

A Computer Help Desk Technician is sometimes called a Help Desk Consultant, or a Help Desk Technical Consultant (if you want to get really formal about it.) The job of a Computer Help Desk Technician is to provide necessary technical expertise to clients who experience problems with the software and/or hardware that the employer of the technician sold or provided to the clients.

A Computer Help Desk Technician may be required to render technical assistance through communication channels such as email and telephone. Usually, the client will call the help desk operations through their telephone landline. The calls are recorded by an automatic call logging system for documentation and review later on.

The Computer Help Desk Technician will have to figure out what are the causes of the problems that the caller is experiencing. For example, if it is a software problem, he may ask questions of the caller to find out if the problems were caused by software glitches, or if there is a virus within the software being used. If it is a hardware problem, the caller may be able to provide clues as to which hardware components seem to be on the fritz.

A Computer Help Desk Technician can help the client even from long distance locations through the wonders of IT advances. For instance, if there is a bug within the software, the Computer Help Desk Technician may be able to notify the Development division so that the bug can be programmed out of the software. If the client found that his data had been corrupted, the Computer Help Desk Technician can help fix the data by dialing into the website of the client.

To be considered for the job of Computer Help Desk Technician, it is not enough to have technical and analytical expertise. One must also possess a pleasant manner on the telephone, a capacity to function even under time pressure, and an ability to work with the team in resolving problems.

What is a Computer Operator Help Desk?

A Computer Operator, first of all, is an employee or staffer of an organization, who has the responsibility of maintaining and running computer systems of the organization on a daily basis, with emphasis on mainframe computer systems. Thus, a Computer Operator Help Desk could be said to mean a Help Desk Network that is staffed by Computer Operators who have the complicated task of assisting clients with their mainframe computer system problems.

We say that the job of a Computer Operator is complicated because it requires the person to not only possess a high school diploma, but also to the technical knowledge in troubleshooting problems with software and hardware; batch-process monitoring; system performance maintenance and enhancement; increasing online availability; and systems and applications documentation maintenance. Other duties that the employer might add on to the job description of a Computer Operator Help Desk staff are: system backups; computer room equipment maintenance (inclusive of tape storage gadgets and printers); and even supplying customer support of some kind.

It is important that Computer Operator Help Desk staff be able to absorb much (if not all) technical knowledge about applications favored by the employer, how to run local area networks, and operating systems being used in the organization. The Computer Operator can be called a member of the Technical Support Staff, and may be known by other job titles such as: Help Desk Staff, Tech Support, Computer Operators, Technical Trainers, Technical Support Engineers, PC Support Staff, Technical Support Specialists, Trainers, Technicians, and PC Technicians.

Specific skills required for the job are: capacity to follow technical instructions to the letter; assess problems and situations encountered so that a corresponding plan of action can be drafted and implemented; as well as in-depth knowledge of the specific system or technology being used.

What Do We Mean By Desktop Help Desk Network LAN Tech Support PC Tech?

The convoluted term Desktop Help Desk Network LAN Tech Support PC Tech may be quite a mouthful to speak, but it need not be confusing. To understand it, one must break it down into its components so you can comprehend their semantics.

LAN Tech Support means the providing of technical expertise via technical support to Local Area Networks (or LAN's). This means LAN Tech Support staff members have to know how to provide maintenance and technical expertise about Computer Networks in particular.

PC Tech, of course, means technology about personal computers. So, a person who knows PC Tech can help in providing maintenance and technical knowledge about personal computers.

A desktop Help Desk Network is another matter altogether. It refers to the use of desktop computers (such as the ubiquitous personal computer sitting on your desk) to provide support assistance to the Help Desk Network. A Help Desk Network is the phone-in system that allows customers to call technicians about their problems with the software and/or hardware they are using. A desktop Help Desk Network may use traditional routing systems (such as cables) to deliver data to each desktop terminal, and to the Help Desk Network administrator; or remote access technology can also be used so that the desktop Help Desk Network may be used even when people switch desks, or are far from their regular locations.

Thus, when all these terms are taken together, the whole term Desktop Help Desk Network LAN Tech Support PC Tech can be seen to mean that this is a Help Desk Network that functions from desktop workstations (either via traditional cable linkages or remote access technology), whose main function is to provide technical support about Local Area Networks with emphasis on the personal computer components.

Good For Us, We Have Front Desk Help, the Heroic Front Liners.

In this software-dependent world, with modern technological advances, everything seems to have to be done with speed and accuracy. However, nothing invented so far can perfectly replace human capabilities in knowing the nuances of interacting with other people. The front desk help can be said to be the front liners of the company, and they deal directly with customer queries and complaints. It is said that when a call is dropped, the caller will be so unhappy with the service, he will initiate a return call. Front desk help must be equipped to handle calls with authority, speed and accuracy using the resources at hand. In this regard, it is necessary to have well-trained personnel who know how to manage and juggle knowledge and problem resolution tools (also called technology).

There are several tools and resources available that are designed to assist the front desk help team. These are help desk software that you find in the IT market today. Such software could include self-help materials too. However, it is still necessary for the user to be knowledgeable about how to maximize the efficiency of the software. The most important features of this tool are the solid call tracking and management capabilities. No matter how the software is designed, the bottom line is that it should be able to assist the team in quickly resolving the callers' problems.

Front desk help staff must be experts in the ins and outs of the system and capable of troubleshooting (meaning they can diagnose and treat problems simultaneously). This kind of technology can be used for both basic and complex problems that may arise. It is up to the front desk team to implement the technology as they see fit. The goal of this department, after all, is to maintain customer satisfaction by guaranteeing swift action on any concerns.

The Relationship Between Help And Desk And Representative

We all know what a help desk representative is; that is the person who mans the help desk system for your IT company. But, what is the relationship between help and desk and representative?

Your help desk representative is the one who recognizes the moment when users are most receptive to learn about how they can help themselves the next time the same problem happens. This is where the term help in help desk representative comes from; meaning, you assist the customer. IT support representatives must be able to cope with frustration expressed against them professionally and keep their cool even under stress.

The desk in the term help desk representative indicates that your technical representatives have skills and know what it takes to deliver quality service, which puts them in a position of power and authority. Whether your helpdesk provides IT support to internal users or your field service engineer problem solve for external customers, your team should be able to communicate their expertise and technical proficiency in a way that will bring respect for people in their position.

The last word is representative, meaning your technical staff serve as ambassadors of technical knowledge and goodwill to internal and external users of the help desk service. Thus, your help desk representative should satisfy customer needs so that users remain loyal to your organization. This depends on how consistent, customer-focused, productive and competitive your internal and external help desks are. Your technical staff should bear in mind that they are front-liners, so their attitude and behavior may imply how the rest of the organization perceives customers.

The help desk needs to identify areas for improvement in skills, customize program content to meet service goals, and improve team performance. Yet, they must also maintain consistency through best practices skills training and on-the-job experience. This helps save time and money for both the service provider and the clients. At the same time, it reduces frustration in customers and fosters loyalty from them as well.

Defining Help Desk Customer Service

To increase customer satisfaction, confidence in your firm, and respect for your help desk customer service, you must provide user-friendly customer service, while delivering technical support to the customer. It is imperative to assign highly qualified help desk staff who possess customer service skills. They must also provide professional technical support skills to the IT support system, which is the help desk customer service system. Choose agents who are more capable of providing necessary solutions to software problems, this is a basic customer service challenge.

To strengthen your reputation as a quality service provider, you ought to evaluate the user-friendliness and effectiveness of your IT help desk to meet your standards for customer service (or even make them better). Your help desk staff should always respect the customer, yet adhere to the highest levels of technical support. This means handling calls efficiently, while providing precise information. It is also important that your technical professionals can interact with users to minimize their frustration, recognize the causes of the problems that lead to queries, suggest applicable solutions, and educate your customers in a polite way.

Take time to mull over the efficiency of your technical support system (looking beyond your present knee-jerk eagerness to provide customer satisfaction). Technical support representatives should be able to resolve issues while on call. This involves guiding customers tactfully and efficiently from feelings of frustration to problem-solving mode.

Aside from that, your company should rate the help desk to ensure the capacity of the staff to do the job. Evaluate your staff regarding their ability to raise call levels according to priority, while maintaining the confidence of the user in their capacity to take action on the present and potential problems before the caller hangs up.

Technical support requires a good balance of technical skill and communication, and also involves interpersonal skills; because the technical staff is responsible for maintaining your standards in customer service. You may find that your help desk customer service staff may need to undergo refresher courses on advanced customer service, so that service is consistent at all times. Technical training will help them deal with difficult situations arising out of obscure questions and weird problems set before them by callers.

The Importance of Help Desk Desktop Support

Got desktop problems? Scratching your head due to desktop troubles you can't seem to figure out? Not to worry, because we are in the 21st century where all technical difficulties can theoretically be answered. You do not need to force yourself to understand desktop problems beyond your abilities, because there are people who are just a call away, who can help you.

Just like every other human invention, desktop PCs are not made as self-maintaining devices. From time to time, your desktop PC needs help being cleaned, polished and refreshed inside and out. There will come a time when it will malfunction, or perhaps completely break down. Not all people are clever at fixing them, so that is where desktop support comes in.

The help desk desktop support can give nationwide or even worldwide access regarding desktop service, technical support and repair. Support basically means to help you out when problems occur, and you cannot find solutions on your own. This is their job, to find solutions for you. Often, mistakes occur due to lack of in-depth understanding about your PC. When this happens, these people are always there to help you repair your computer, and may even teach you how to do it yourself.

Desktop support is manned by people who are often not thanked enough for their work, yet are still happy to continue with this type of service. There are times when the PC users who call in to the help desk support system may become frustrated and even verbally abusive, yet the help desk desktop support staff is obliged to be courteous under fire. They are workers who are often not recognized for the work they have done, but still continue to serve successive batches of customers who need assistance with their PC.

Why Work At a Help Desk in New York City?

A help desk at a call center nowadays presents global job opportunities for people who are highly skilled in the advancing field of information technology. As the computer age peaks within our time, we are seeing more and more computer problems cropping up and frustrating end users. This is why a help desk in New York City, which is an example of a place where using computers has become a way of life for residents, has become a necessary service.

As we absorb technology into our lives, it becomes necessary to get more help from people who have more talents and skills at maintaining and troubleshooting computers. In New York City alone, you can find people who are very dependent on their laptops and PCs for work, leisure and family activities. Thus, you need not wonder why help desk job opportunities have grown in the city.

Can you think of anyone who would not grab the golden opportunity of earning a good salary, with valuable health and dental benefits thrown in, when they answer ads for call center agents? Considering the great working environment as well, New Yorkers would definitely consider a job in help desk assistance any day.

You should not think that a help desk in New York City is solely for highly skilled computer support agents. There are actually many other call center opportunities available there. Some advertise about help desk jobs for automotive specialists; market agents involved in sales, particularly outbound calls; travel guides; location listings; and even stock market assistance, among many others. Indeed, working at help desk jobs means having your world opened to a wide range of interests and occupations.

This type of job offers a salary that varies with the experience you have when you apply, and after you've worked for that employer for some time. Given that you stand to earn benefits such as paid sick leave, most people who are hunting for the right job may want to consider the call center work to make a living.

Seeing yourself as a help desk staffer means working in a job that is a very admirable service. You help others, such as callers, and are able to relieve the burden of looking for the information they need.

What Does Help Desk Level 1 Status Mean?

In the world of information technology, IT companies (both large and small) are expected to maintain call-center help desks that assist customers with any problems that they might encounter. To make such call-center help desks function better, and relieve the pressure on help desk technicians, it is necessary to maintain a call-level system so that the help desk staff prioritize calls based on how urgent and important they are. This is where the Help Desk Level 1 officer comes in.

A Help Desk Level 1 officer is responsible for problems that need a fast first level of response. The Help Desk Level 1 officer is supported by Help Desk Level 2, and Help Desk Level 3 staffers. Help Desk Level 1 personnel are necessary to an IT service company because they can reassure callers who are worried that their problems might be placed on the backburner by the help desk operations of the call center.

When the IT company uses a call-level system, there are benefits that come with it, such as:

1. reduction of delays and handoffs, since callers are led to the best resource within the help desk operations;
2. permitting IT technicians on the job to examine how complex problems that callers experienced were eventually resolved (either by Help Desk Level 1 people, or their support staff at the Help Desk Level 2 and 3);
3. allowing intake staff to examine the causes of problems called in, so that future callers may be given solutions that have worked for previous callers;
4. call center staff who have higher positions can concentrate on management and administrative responsibilities rather than have to deal with front liner issues themselves.

How Does a Help Desk PC Call Center Handle Angry Callers?

So, you entered a call center as a help desk staff for personal computer and computer concerns; and boy, do you feel proud of yourself. Until, on your first day on the job, when you get a call from a very, very angry customer who apparently is not in the mood to recognize you as a professional help desk staffer. So, how does a help desk PC call center agent handle angry callers like this?

First, never take anything the callers say personally. That is the main thing you should remember when you get an angry caller. Take deep breaths if necessary to calm yourself down, and try to stay focused on diagnosing the problem presented to you.

Second, use statements that are known to help calm down the other party, like: "I Understand Where You Are Coming From With This;" or, "I Think I See What The Problem Is."

Third, wait out the tirade of the caller before proposing a solution. Yes, this means having a massive storehouse of patience (as well as tough ears) to withstand all that yelling and cursing, but that is what professionalism is all about.

Then, try to let the client know that you empathize with their circumstances. If the problem is really complex, that may explain why the client feels so frustrated. Honey attracts more flies than vinegar, so it doesn't help if you become sarcastic as well (not to mention you might find yourself out of a job if you resort to that.)

If you see that your organization is truly at fault (maybe because the defect cited by the caller is a production-related defect), then you might try apologizing for the inconvenience. Unless, of course, there are legal restrictions in your contract as a help desk staffer that prohibit you from admitting fault for the company, until a supervisor or legal counsel can examine the case.

Angry callers are part and parcel to the life of a help desk technical support staff. So, do your best to keep your cool, and do your job the way you were trained to do it.

Do I Need a Help Desk PC Technician?

A personal computer nowadays has become a normal part of everyday lives. For the present generation, it has also become quite common for a person to worry about computer problems that they cannot fix by themselves. Not everyone has the necessary skills to maintain personal computers. Those who are blessed with such skills may be found working 24 hours a day to help people out with their computer-related problems. Such people may hold the title of Help Desk PC technician (though they may also be known by other names that all mean the same thing.)

Often, the average person may not understand what a computer malfunction may be due to, simply because they lack adequate knowledge. On the other hand, PC technicians do have that knowledge, so they can help you out. You need not invite help desk PC technicians into your home (which lots of people would prefer not doing). The Help Desk PC Technician you contact at the Help Desk Network will talk to you while you follow their detailed instructions. You should view this as an opportunity for you to get to know more about your PC. With the knowledge imparted by the Help Desk PC Technician, perhaps one day you can help a friend when they encounter the same problem(s) you already fixed.

There are many types of help desk PC technicians to be found, simply because there are so many manufacturers of PCs nowadays. If they need to visit your home to get a closer look at your PC, this requires scheduling and appointments at your and their convenience. Some common problems that they deal with are virus infection, spyware removal, unexplained changes in the performance of your PC, slow computer activity, pop-ups, networking issues, and many more.

You do not need to worry that you will be humiliated by the professionals in the business. It is the non-professionals you should be cautious about. This is why it is important to tap PC technicians who are connected with a reputable IT organization, because those types of employees are required to maintain professionalism in all their dealings with customers and the public.

Treat Your Help Desk Support Specialist As Your First Line of Defense.

The help desk support specialist team is the first group in the company who are in a position to assist customers in any way necessary. There are several basic steps these employees must follow in dealing with customers.

First, they must try to categorize the problem, from simple ones (which can be easily solved) to complex issues (those that need in-depth technical support). The company is fully dependent on its help desk support specialist team in this respect, so they can handle and resolve the complaint immediately.

Second, the team must try to solve the problem using available resources, and their inherent expertise. However, the help desk support specialist team should not attempt to do more than they can handle. If you (the specialist) find it too hard to solve a problem, elevate the call to the right department or person for further action.

The help desk support specialist team must make use of available organizational resources such as modern troubleshooting support, technicians, librarians and software consultants, to name a few.

Any help desk support specialist must be able to identify which is the right department to refer the client to if the problem is quite complicated or serious. Proper endorsement of the customer is necessary.

The team must realize that the essence of being a help desk support specialist is to be able to provide the necessary support service that includes immediate troubleshooting of the perceived problem.

The success of a help desk support specialist does not necessarily revolve around successful troubleshooting of the problem. Simply treating the customer with respect, and then referring him to the right team or department is already good performance. Guaranteeing that the customer is satisfied with the assistance he receives will spell the difference between a return call and a satisfied customer. This is possible only if the team is well trained, and is equipped to handle any type of customer and problem. We can see then that the impression customers have about the company is very much dependent on how the help desk support specialist team treats them.

Thanks for Help Desk Tech Support

What is help desk tech support? It is basically a group of people with a host of information technology skills that can help you with your IT-related problems with just one phone call. There are many types of help desk tech support, but all of them have the commonality with other tech support of helping those who are not skilled enough to perform PC troubleshooting.

Help desk tech support staff are technical support agents who can assist you in sorting out hardware or software technicalities. They can solve your PC problems directly; if not, they will transfer you to someone else in the technical support team that they know can be of better assistance. They will persist in their service until your problems are thoroughly resolved. While on duty, they will try to resolve as many questions as possible for as many people as can reasonably be handled.

Calling help desk tech support is much cheaper than having a computer technician come into your home, and is also less invasive, as far as privacy is concerned. The vast technological changes we face today make it important to have people skilled in information technology. They lend a helping hand to those who have less knowledge or skills with computers. It is nice that there are help desk tech support nowadays who also teach callers how to solve problems that crop up. As a result, they need not call the help desk tech support every time they experience PC-related problems.

Some people may become so dependent on help desk tech support that even minor problems, that do not really require the help of the technical support staff, are called in. When this happens, the help desk tech support is still expected to be the professionals that they are, and must coach these types of callers with skill and much patience. They should also impart confidence to their callers so that the latter will be able to solve their problems by themselves, when these same problems crop up again.

The Problem With the Help Desk Telecommute System

Let us first examine what the word telecommute is all about. Telecommuters are people who work in different occupations that all have to do with helping people somehow. The big difference is they work from home or from remote locations outside a traditional office. A help desk telecommute system then, is a help desk system maintained by the employer of these telecommuters to assist such employees in their work. Thus they can function outside the traditional workplace just as efficiently as traditional workers.

One example of a telecommuter would be people who work for government agencies in the US. Many government agencies are opting to let their employees become telecommuters (or simply home-based workers). However, though it may seem that becoming a telecommuter would be beneficial to everyone concerned, actually, the employee may be on the losing end (depending on how his employer approaches the help desk telecommute service).

It goes this way: the employer (perhaps a government agency) permits employees to become telecommuters primarily because the employer wants to save money. But, to save a lot of money, the employer may require the employee to purchase his own computer, which the employer will say should only be used for the particular occupation they are in. It is advisable for such employees to invest in laptops so they can work from different locations, if necessary. The employer will then maintain a help desk for such telecommuters so that they can iron out any problems they encounter with their business-only computer.

Problems with this so-called perfect help desk telecommute system crop up when the employee installs unapproved software into his business-only computer. So, when he calls the help desk, the help desk personnel find it harder to help the employee because he used software that does not have any business use. For example, some employees will install games into their business-only computer. That kind of violation can cost the employee his job in the end, or at the very least, a black mark on his employment record.

Hewlett Packard Comes Out With HP Help Desk Services

Hewlett Packard is known for creating printers that do a great job for home-based and traditional employees alike. But now, Hewlett Packard is also accepting outsourced contracts to supply the service desk services of client companies. Hewlett Packard calls this function the HP Service Desk (or HP Help Desk) service.

Outsourcing helps many companies who do not consider Information Technology to be their core competency. These client companies can outsource their HP Service Desk needs to the Hewlett Packard Company, so that they can lessen the burden on their in-house IT personnel. Thus they become more flexible with their business functions, and reap cost savings in the process. Hewlett Packard offers both customer and standard service desk packages to client companies.

When a client company or client organization allows it help desk function to be shouldered by Hewlett Packard through its HP Help Desk service, the client organization is able to stay flexible enough to adjust to a fluctuating business environment. They also enhance the efficiency of their IT people, as well as the productivity of end-users. This makes the support system less complicated to deal with by both the management of the client organization and the end-users. They can then manage existing costs and predict future expenses, hike service response and resolution speed. This permits their in-house IT department to concentrate on making the core competencies of the client organization function better and improve it over time.

Why should a client organization choose to outsource to Hewlett Packard, among all the other possible choices? Hewlett Packard is competent at workplace outsourcing (as perceived by reputable analysts such as Forrester and META Group). Hewlett Packard relies only on best practices at industry standard level for its IT service management functions.

What is a Network Help Desk Responsible for?

When we refer to the term help desk, it implies support services rendered by a group of highly qualified people, who work to help people who feel lost when confronted with technical problems and situations. Help desks are not all alike. For instance, a PC help desk is different from a network help desk. A PC help desk involves technical information within the realm of personal computers. A network help desk work involves the technology of computer networking.

What is networking? Networking consists of multiple computer systems linked together in some way. The formal definition is that a network is a chain of computers joined together in a certain pattern or design that exchange information by communicating with each other. There are many options on how a network can be formed. It can be done by linking cables, radio waves, telephone lines, infrared and Bluetooth, and satellite. There are three (3) basic network types: LAN (local area network) for small areas such as home-based offices and small companies; MAN (metropolitan area network) for districts or cities that need to be interconnected within a large area; and WAN (wide area network), which allows connectivity within states or between countries.

A network help desk assists with connectivity problems. This means they solve problems that occur within the network such as trouble accessing the Internet, when Internet access is possible, but the user cannot log into their networking chat rooms, common IP addressing problems, bad cabling, and poor connection speed, among others.

The similarities between a network help desk and a PC help desk are that they provide assistance to callers using landlines twenty-four (24) hours a day, seven (7) days a week, and they both employ people who are very skilled and knowledgeable about computer systems to take your call.

The Indispensable PC Help Desk Support.

With all the current technological advances, we know technology has no way to go but forward. In order for companies to stay competitive, they need to find ways to pamper clients by offering fast action to address their problems. This is why PC help desk support was created.

Selling or closing a sale does not mean the end of the relationship between the company and the customer; actually, it is just the beginning. Aside from answering questions about the product the customer has bought, the PC help desk support may tackle possible complaints (mostly technical in nature) about the functionality of the product, or the usual queries about the warranties do or do not cover.

With the use of the PC Help Desk support, we now have the technology to address such problems. Help desk support is available to customers 24/7, and more importantly, is only a phone call away. The help desk support team is there so that the help desk can identify and solve user problems through remote capabilities. They provide complete instructions, and immediately dispatch a field technician or engineer to fix the problem, when necessary. they also serve as the central point of contact between the company and the customer; train the customer in simple upkeep and troubleshooting of problems, while also providing the customer with updates or advanced engineering support.

Help desk support is an indispensable part of the company, since it also supports the sales department. The help desk can provide tracking reports or data problem reports. It is the team that supplies the company with a series of activities essential for monitoring and updates. Lastly, customers gain a sense of security regarding their needs when the help desk is on the job.

What Does It Take to Become A Supervisor Analyst Help Desk Operations Trucking Logistics Officer?

Before we can delve into what it takes to become a supervisor analyst help desk operations trucking logistics, it is necessary to break down that job title into its elements, so we can understand what we are talking about.

Trucking logistics is basically an industry devoted to the transportation of merchandise through vast geographical regions with the help of organizational logistics support, such as advanced technology. At present, the vast industry of logistics is believed to contribute around $1.06 trillion into the US gross domestic product. Even with the slowdown of the US economy right now, third-party logistics companies were able to hike their total revenue by 24% as of year 2000 to the $56.4-billion mark. That is how great business is at present for logistics companies. Trucking service makes up a major part of the logistics industry, with 80 cents out of every dollar funneled toward freight shipping used for trucking as the means of transportation.

Then what are help desk operations, in that case? As the term implies, help desk operations do just that; provide help to people who encounter problems with the respective service they were trying to avail themselves of. In this case, we are talking about help desk operations for trucking logistics, so logically that means the help desk operations will help in resolving any problems you might encounter using trucking logistics. Help desk operations vary, from maintaining round-the-clock phone lines staffed by help desk call center staff, to self-service forms on the website of the trucking logistics company.

Onward to the supervisor analyst term. This indicates that this is the person in charge of the following functions for the trucking logistics help desk operations: monitoring vendor information requests; serve as liaison among the areas of finance, buyers and vendors; and also determine the location policies for the warehousing system (among many other functions.)

The Finer Points of Web based Help Desk Systems

When we say we are using a web-based system, it means it is a system utilized by the service provider through a web-based application. This indicates that the programs used for the web-based system can be run through a web server and web pages. Through the help of such tools, the user and the target clients can select the best web-based software that they want to use. Thus, a web-based help desk can help introduce users and clients as to which software is most reliable, which can be purchased at a much lower price, and which offers better quality. And all comparable to the different varieties of desktop software in the market.

Often, the web-based software requires a much more limited number of programmers, or help desk representatives, to assist you (the end user or client); if compared to a medium-sized desktop software project that employs over a hundred personnel who man that unit of their department. It is clearly more advantageous for companies to adopt web-based application software.

Actually, most users do not seem to care, or perhaps just ignore the significance of, choosing the best web-based software for their purposes. Perhaps this is because web-based applications seem to be provided so easily that they are taken for granted. To utilize a web-based application, you can just ask your help desk representative to connect your browser to the Internet. And the web-based application can be used anywhere, as long as there is an available service provider or network.

You might find it beneficial that with the web-based software your data and application remain intact, even when problems crop up such as interruption of network operations. So, you do not have to install anything to use it, which makes life simpler for you. And when there is no installation taking place, that is one less thing to worry about. Your help desk representative will help you resolve any problems encountered using the Web-based application, and in your operating system (particularly when the software malfunctions.)

With web-based applications, it is much easier for the help desk representative and the users to use the same version. Bugs can be fixed as soon as they are discovered, because web-based software usually has fewer bugs than desktop software.

Furthermore, web-based applications can be used by several people at the same time, and your data will be safer or at least protected. This means the software is less vulnerable to invasion by viruses or bugs.

Why IT Organizations Should Invest in Computer Help Desk Software

Various computer help desk systems nowadays function on a sharp learning curve, just so they can provide great support to their customers. To address any dilemmas brought about by technical deficiencies in the software system purchased or made for the customers, some companies are now vigilant in adopting the best computer help desk software that can really satisfy the needs of their customers. Some companies used to adapt the customer service trouble ticket system in their operations. This trouble ticket system requires new users to be trained, but it is considered an instinctive, well-designed screen layout that makes the system easy for operators.

Your computer help desk must be consistent in taking action when technical troubles are correspondingly backed up by call reports from a client (which must include the personal identification of the client as well). When there is a history of unresolved calls, the help desk must take note of the priority rating monitored by the client logging call system, so that the operators can easily see the status of any unresolved calls at any point in the process.

You might find also that with this system, the users can easily manage any calls assigned to them; proven by the fact that the operator can easily act on or resolve the queries of the client. But if the operator is unable to resolve the problem, he can refer the call to another operator.

It is necessary for the help desk system and the operator to have the right web browser to log in a new support call. This allows them to immediately interface with the system anywhere (because the system is web-based). The help desk operation is held responsible for assuring the clients and users that they have the available resources to provide a good support service, and improve over time, if necessary.

The helpdesk software will give you guaranteed service and may even pay you double your money back, if needed. This is why the computer operator should be well trained in giving support to customers, coupled with excellent customer service.

Computer help desk software helps your users and customers save money and time while rendering the best service they can. When the organization is able to provide a computer system that is easy to set up and use, yet remains accessible from virtually anywhere, then that is a powerful help desk system, and the organization can easily afford to invest in it.

How to Prepare for a Career as a Computer Network Help Desk Technician

Do you like computers? If yes, to what degree do you like them? Just a little, a lot, or are you the type of person who cannot exist if you are not tinkering with computers? If you answered yes to the last description, then maybe you have what it takes to become a Computer Network Help Desk Technician.

To get started as a Computer Network Help Desk Technician, you need to have at least a diploma in that field. There are many credible and accredited educational institutions from which you can earn that degree. Once you have that diploma, it is easy to apply for any one of the following jobs: computer support technician, call center support technician, or help desk support technician. All three job titles mean that you will serve as a technical expert in the computer network help desk that help end users.

While studying for your diploma, you will gain experience and technical knowledge about how to install, troubleshoot, and maintain personal computers; management of computer networks, and providing desktop support for Microsoft Windows operating environments. Of particular importance in this field is knowing how to deal with the Windows-based applications and operating systems (with emphasis on installation, management and repair).

You may be wondering why you need a diploma to become a Computer Network Help Desk Technician, rather than work for a BA or BS degree instead (such as BS Computer Science). The truth behind the matter is that the jobs you will be applying for do not really need the higher-level qualifications inherent in BA or BS degrees. You will be valued more for your technical know-how in computers, rather than for having a more comprehensive education. However, if you should desire to upgrade your educational qualifications while working as a Computer Help Desk Technician, it is always possible to apply for distance learning options in the Continuing Education programs of certain institutions.

What Kind of Service Should I Expect From The Dell Help Desk?

With the fast pace of the introduction of technological advances, computers are now known as a major element in our daily lives. We use computers all the time: at work, in our homes, and even in our schools. We see that technology is now commonly used, not just by adults but even children. However there is another trend accompanying these developments as well; computer-related problems have also become quite prevalent. Using these machines regrettably brings trouble as well as convenience.

Though you may consider yourself skillful when it comes to your PC, there are still problems that are best left to the experts. This is why we try to call people we believe can resolve our computer-related problems. Such people can be found manning PC help desks 24 hours a day, 7 days a week.

Some of these PC competent people would be the Dell technical support team. In the US alone, there are numerous 1-800 numbers maintained by the Dell IT company. They form support teams in different user categories for your convenience; such as the categories of home, home office, small, medium and large business, state and local government, federal government, health care, k-12 education, higher education, and speech and hearing impairment.

If you feel comfortable with the idea of talking with a call center agent, Dell has a help desk system staffed with bi-lingual agents for people from different ethnic groups. Spanish and French are some of the most common languages spoken by call center agents (aside from the usual English language, which is the current lingua franca of the world).

What makes the Dell help desk different from other help desks you can find is that it offers not only phone-based support, but also provides online means as well through Internet chat rooms, and via email.

Still, the Dell help desk is similar to other help desks in that it offers the services of their technical support teams 24 hours a day, 7 days a week, even on holidays. Customers may rest assured that agents from Dell are properly trained, and adhere to the highest skills standards.

Understanding What Desktop Help Desk Software Has to Offer Customers

Before you can understand what desktop help desk software is, you need to understand its core terms: Help Desk Software. Basically, help desk software is a help desk system that operates either through your desktop workstation or through web-based applications. The help desk software that can be run via desktop workstations is dubbed desktop help desk software, while help desk software that is dependent on web-based applications is called web-based help desk software.

Some features that desktop help desk software are known for would be an ability to create a host of reports, contract management functions, knowledgebase, email logging, email notification, and of course, the necessary web interface. Each desktop workstation could be connected to the network via conventional access (meaning cable infrastructure) or through remote access (which means you could even move your desktop computer to different locations and you would still be connected to the system).

Desktop help desk software can also be designed to assist help desk support staff, when they are trying to diagnose the problems encountered by desktop computer users. This desktop help desk software system is used by the help desk department of a particular organization. It will itself require continuous maintenance, and management, and even occasional or periodic upgrades; if that help desk department is to stay on top of its technical support functions. It is important that the help desk department rely on best practice strategies to manage its responsibilities.

Why is it important to use appropriate desktop help desk software? Aside from the obvious benefits to customers (the callers), the organization running the help desk department itself will be able to avoid running astronomical costs linked to calls and incidents. Some experts price the process of problem resolution per caller at $14 to $18, while each incident necessitating a higher level of help desk support may run to as high as $90 per incident. It is believed using the right desktop help desk software may mitigate such expenses on a cumulative basis.

Reasons Why Your Business Needs Desktop Support and Help Desk Administration

Technology has indeed come a long way. Computer programs upgrade faster than you could ever imagine. Good thing there are desktop support and help desk administration that can help you with troubleshooting. Whether it is PC, Linux, Macintosh or even Unix, their professional desktop support can help you with your problems.

Companies, especially computer shops and other software companies, have desktop support and help desk administration to help first time users. Others have a hard time fixing and figuring out the programs. And, most people who buy software programs have a hard time installing and making them work.

Service they offer:

Some service providers and companies offer warranties that can replace parts in 24 hours. This kind of service is included in desktop support. Experienced technicians are there to help the clients. This support is very essential if you have a business. Using the software and programs to communicate and operate your business is a vital element. Help desks and desktop support will help you figure out the techniques and solution to your query.

Help desk administration, on the other hand, gives you the support that you need. Just like the usual job of help desk, they are the ones who assist and facilitate gathering of information and details. They support and answer, and follow up the queries of your clients. Help desk administration also enters various data to update the clients with the latest advice and support.

Desktop support and help desk administration work hand in hand in creating a successful business with happy and satisfied customers. Remember that customer inquiries are important in keeping a good reputation for your company. You have to realize that without the help of desktop support and help desk administration, you will have to go through each question and inquiry of your customers. Moreover, help desk will support, update and improve customer service in your business.

Work of an Entry Level Help Desk Employee

Problems posed to the support help desk need to be resolved immediately. The level of support provided depends on the degree of the problem seeking solutions. The first level of support is expected to give immediate solutions to problems relating to basic questions about the application system, or error message encountered, and specific events that transpired prior to the problem. Solutions to some of these problems may be referenced from the help desk database or other documentation, or through consulting a colleague.

The entry-level help desk employee should have a strong knowledge of the system and software applications. Title positions given to an entry-level help desk staffer may be: Desktop Technician, Help Desk Technician, Technical Support Agent, and Technical Customer Service Representative. Their duties involve answering telephone calls, analyzing problems based on the automated diagnostic programs, and resolving recurring issues. The entry-level help desk employee should be detail-oriented, a good problem solver, have good communication/people skills, and be strongly team-orientation.

An entry-level help desk position provides opportunity for an individual to get to the 2nd level of support. As they hone their knowledge and experience, they move to an advanced position in the support help desk. Their advanced knowledge and experience may lead them to becoming network administrators, application developers, and/or database administrators. The salary of an entry-level help desk employee ranges from $35,000 to $45,000 annually.

Being in the entry-level help desk, you become the initial troubleshooter for your organization. As you deal directly with customer issues, your utmost concern is the handling of the issues in a professional manner, and this is what is expected of you.

Gain Entry to the IT World Through the Entry-Level in a Junior Level Help Desk Support Position

You have earned considerable education and training in preparation for a career in the IT world; it is now time to pursue that dream. It may occur to you to question how you will go about doing that exactly. Here are some guidelines you can use so that you can get into the first level of employment, which is entry-level as a junior help desk support staffer.

When you are in the junior level help desk support position, you are expected to be willing to learn more about the IT field. The experience you gain in help desk support will provide you with basic to advanced knowledge of the help desk world.

Occasionally, you may feel jittery (which is normal when working in a new job). Just keep your focus on showing that you are competent in your job. And, while you do your job, you must try to maintain a good working relationship with clients, callers, and the people you work with.

Your basic responsibility as part of help desk support would be answering calls about problems encountered by the callers. Try not to let any caller down, meaning that you should attend to all problems swiftly, yet as accurately as you can. Know your limitations, so that you do not try to troubleshoot problems beyond your capabilities. Always ask for support or assistance from team members when very complicated problems are presented to you. Your level of technical knowledge may bring you to the junior entry level. however, to go further, and last the race, you must handle customers and their concerns properly. Also, cooperate with team members, and generally show that you are very competent in the challenging world of advanced information technology systems.

Role of the Help Desk Desktop 3rd Level

In a help desk support, there are three levels where support requests of customers are handled. These levels of support are as follows:

1. First level Support handles problems and questions of customers. It provides customers the solution to their problems through the basic application of the system and/or hardware assistance. An electronic Help Desk will answer the call. Through the use of a case-based reasoning system the customer is able to have an automatic interface with the system.

2. Second Level Support deals with problems that cannot be resolved at the first level. A Technical Analyst handles these cases. He or she provide more complex support, and application software and hardware expertise solution to callers.

3. Third Level Support deals with problems that cannot be resolved at the 2nd level. Most of the common problems are software bugs that require a review of the programming.

Of the three (3) levels of support, the help desk desktop 3rd level is the most critical that needs immediate attention. The need for core experts at this level is a must. It is expected that these experts will develop, research and provide support services such as hardware repair, email, networking, telephone, and client-server applications. The third level support is for companies with limited IT staff, or where a network administrator support presence is required. Most of the common problems handled are with Advanced Configuration Management.

At the 3rd level, a high demand of positive outcomes is expected by the organization. Thus, a comprehensive report should be provided from the first level up to the third, to have the business operation run continuous and smooth. Keep customers happy by providing them the ultimate satisfaction.

Help Desk PC Support to Answer Your Needs

As human beings are composed of mind and body, so are computer made up of software and hardware. Inasmuch as computers are man-made and may either breakdown or malfunction, they will need "medical" attention as surely as their human operators. Technicians are the knights in shining armor on their white horses that ride to the rescue of users having difficulty with their PC.

In today's advanced technology, help desk PC support is available for users to address their concerns or inquiries. When customers find problems with their PC, the very first thing that comes to their mind is to call the PC support. At most times, lack of understanding of the operational features of the PC is generally assumed to be the cause of the breakdown, and the call support brings that to the attention of the user. The help desk PC support also allows organizations to immediately answer inquiries on a 24/7 basis, thus providing a high quality of service to customers. The help desk PC support allows your customers and technicians to have Internet connection, and access to the web browser. Customers and technicians can communicate online and tackle the problem at hand via a one on one conversation. The help desk PC support is designed for the Internet and Intranet logging into anywhere. It does not limit you from hiring technicians, even from remote places. The help desk PC support provides automatic notification to technicians through email or pager, to look into a support problem immediately. Its database is fully searchable, and also includes customer history, tons of statistics, and much more. A help desk PC support screens problems, and sends problems to the appropriate department to handle the request.

Reducing the handling times of finding solutions for your customers is the goal of your help desk PC support. Make it your tool to start building good, solid relationships with your clients.

Help Desk: How to Troubleshoot With Your Client

Firms today depend more on help desk. This amazing concept is a great tool to support users and customers. Most companies offer support to customers through toll free numbers, and others through emails and websites. In-house help desks are also giving the same support to different departments. There are schools that provide the skills to create solutions to technical problems.

Help desks have quite a lot of responsibilities and functions. They supply the users with vital information on computer issues and queries. The help desk deals with its clients by using software that will facilitate these inquiries. Tracking systems are usually used by delivery systems that provide the client a ticket number. In this way, it is easier and faster to work with the inquires that people make every day. The help desk does not only provide you with all the technical answers, but it also evaluates the problem. The customer informs the help desk of their questions and complaints while the help desk provides a tracking number / ticket. If the problem is resolved, then the ticket is set to be closed.

There are huge help desks that supply and handle all of the inquiries. Help desks answer questions that are commonly asked by users, or what you usually see in the FAQ (frequently asked questions). This is a list of questions that users often ask the company. In this system, you will be able to get the answers to most of your questions. These large help desks have a couple of staff to manage the questions. Basically, larger teams are needed for this kind of help desk structure. They are usually responsible to follow up with the problems, call back the clients, or answer their questions through email.

Help desk is indeed a very important part of each company. Whether it is in-house or a web-based help desk, it is essential to help and support your clients in every way possible.

Do I Qualify as a Help Desk Administrator?

What is a help desk administrator? If you work as a help desk administrator, your job involves acting as the manager of a technical support group known as a help desk. You are needed for the help desk to become fully operational and always functioning in tip-top condition. The help desk team manages the technical system for a client company so that the system will always work and function properly. Help desk administrators are most commonly needed in IT or computer-system service providers, who's PC and network help desks may also be commonly known as call centers.

Before you can become a help desk administrator, you will definitely need a college or university degree with a close relationship to computer science. It is not easy to become a help desk administrator. You will also need years of experience working in the information technology industry so that you know how particular systems work.

To be known as a competent help desk administrator, you should have extensive knowledge about a wide range of different computer systems. If you are considering a career in help desk administration, you should be educated about software, monitoring, maintaining data files, patches, executing backups, and recovering system files (among other diverse skills sets). On the whole, a help desk administrator must be familiar with everything pertaining to computer system management and maintenance.

Administrators are the ones who are responsible for maintaining and systematizing computers to be used by help desk assistants. A help desk administrator should also be creative when it comes to problem solving. In some companies, it is the help desk administrator who is designated as tutor or trainer of new PC help desk agents.

Patience is another quality that an effective help desk administrator should have. Working with people immersed in computer knowledge can be a grueling chore, since you may have to deal with the inflated egos of your staff. Some may not accept what you are trying to implement and become offended. So, as an administrator, you should know how to best phrase any corrections or reprimands you have to dish out.

Still, the salary is considered the best part of becoming a help desk administrator. In fact, many companies are eager to give as much compensation as is demanded by the help desk administrator for his services, no questions asked.

Reasons Why You Need Help Desk Applications in Your Company

In a business, troubleshooting is one thing that needs to be dealt with properly. Your company should be prepared from any queries and setbacks. If your business involves a service industry like communication, food, delivery, and airline service, then you should treat help desk as a serious consideration.

Customer service today has tremendously improved. Technology played a great part in this progress. Now more and more businesses cannot do without help desks in their companies. Industries, organizations and corporations keep on improving customer service. This is to optimize your business system and help your company save money and trouble!

Help desk applications can help your team in your department to maximize your company's potentials. Applications are created primarily to help you answer and satisfy the needs of your clients. Software can assist you in improving your service to your customers. Your work can be done easier. Help desks need a system wherein they can enter essential client information and query. This system can help your department to systematically answer and support your clients.

What are the benefits of help desk applications?

1. They can help you trim down call volumes.
2. You can easily respond to and answer repetitive issues.
3. Staff can provide the support demand, to the client fast and easy. Some systems automatically add the request to the help desk system in their website, which makes it more convenient for the users to an-

swer their questions. This results in less call and wait time.

4. Project mangers and team leaders can track down problems on the product. By reviewing and managing the queues, you will be able to improve your service and your product as well.

Help desk applications can get your company moving in the right direction. This technology can greatly assist you in your business. With less complaints and call volumes, your department and help desk staffs can now handle the complaints effortlessly.

The Downside of Working as a Help Desk Assistant

You may be wondering why some customer service representatives (more commonly known as call center agents) say their job is tiring, stagnant and toxic. Though a help desk assistant such as these people enjoys a high salary commensurate to their skills, and are even provided valuable health benefits and vacations too; some still do not consider this compensation enough motivation for them to continue working as a help desk assistant.

In the US alone, help desks or call centers created 5 million jobs back in the 1990s. That was when call center jobs became some of the most sought-after in the world. However, because the nature of the work of a help desk assistant demands flexible working hours, graveyard shifts, and a willingness to work even on holidays, this places a significant burden on the employees (who already have to solve difficult problems for callers).

There are call centers that simply shutdown eventually for various reasons. For instance, some help desk assistants did not undergo further training, after being employed by the call center. This resulted in stagnation of their communication skills. Others lost their enthusiasm for their work after doing the same duties for the employer day-in, day-out. Some customer representatives resented being called agents. Time pressure may affect the performance of agents who are trying to match standards for technical skills set by their company. All of this can be very stressful for the employee whose performance may deteriorate, and result in unresolved calls and bad customer service.

Attrition of call center representatives is a sign of severe pressure from the working conditions, which may result in mental instability. Trying to calm down enraged callers every day, and maintaining long working hours, can really affect your self-esteem after awhile. Even if the help desk assistant has superlative skills for problem-solving technical matters; some callers just do not respect call center agents. Dealing with rude, ill-mannered callers is common throughout the job description of all types of help desk assistants.

Perhaps the key to preventing attrition is to amend company standards, so that call center agents will feel better about themselves and their work, rather than pressuring help desk assistants to adhere to very high (perhaps unreachable) customer service standards.

The Helpdesk Computer is Always on Call

Help desks are a standard in any organization, whether it's for education or professional use. Most establishments offer help-desk support to their clients, either by phone, email, live chat or the Internet. But, it is also common knowledge that employees also need assistance on computer hardware, software and other IT related products and services like network connections, digital media, and many more. It is for this reason that the helpdesk computers were offered by establishments for in-house queries. From basic tasks like how to open or view a file to the more complex troubleshooting of network connections, it can all be found in the computer helpdesk.

In today's fast advancements in technology, many people can't cope with the changes in IT features. It has now become a standard for companies to provide technical assistance to employees through helpdesk computers. The beauty of having a helpdesk computer is that everybody with access to it can avail themselves of the simple help instructions. There is no need for them to dial a number or write an email and wait for someone to answer their questions. Helpdesk computers usually have the answers ready with just the click of a mouse button. They may even have Frequently Asked Questions (or FAQ) links to answer the user's most common inquiries and how-to's. It is available anytime you need it, 24 hours a day and it has no days off.

But, helpdesk computers need not be confined in the organization's office alone. Finding success in helpdesk computers, many websites now offer assistance via the Internet; either for free or for a minimal fee. A simple point-and-click system will help the person understand the technicalities of the product or service he bought. Many sites even offer complete instructions, with either picture or video step-by-step examples to make it easier to understand (even without reading).

So now, it is much easier to get help and answers to almost all of your IT related questions. A helpdesk computer is all you need.

Solutions for Computer IT Hardware

The information age is really at its peak right now. Technology is advancing fast, with new computer hardware being introduced almost every week. With more and more computer IT hardware being released, people will naturally get confused; first timers most especially.

Fortunately, there is hope for those who have little or no experience with computer hardware. A simple search on the net can yield several thousand sites with helpdesks on computer IT hardware. With these helpdesks readily available at the click of a mouse, everything from computer maintenance to troubleshooting and upgrades will be covered, and all for just a minimal fee or sometimes even free! Other topics that can be learned are networking for small, medium and large offices (which will also include troubleshooting and maintenance). They may also offer assistance on media products like digital cameras, DVDs, MP3 players and many other IT hardware products.

We have to admit that not all people are capable of understanding the jargon and hardware involved inside a personal computer. But, with a little study and practice, everyone can be capable of simple computer IT hardware identification and use. This is important because your purchase is your investment, and maximizing investments is what we are all after.

There are helpdesks that specialize solely on computer IT hardware. These helpdesks either have a live chat session with you, or will contact you to assist in whatever IT hardware needs you may have. Some of these helpdesk computer IT hardware specialists also have other services that will cover your business needs as well. These can range from web development and maintenance to taking care of your support group.

Take advantage of easy help online and you'll soon be off to a trouble-free and well-maintained computer.

Help Desk Coordinators: What They Can do for You and Your Business

Help desk coordinators are vital in assisting requests from clients. When you have problems using a particular service, coordinators can aid you in giving the right solution. They are the ones who basically do problem reports from users. Help desk coordinators also execute preliminary analysis and can give you proper support.

Their Main Responsibilities are:

Help desk coordinators receive assistance requests from the customers. Their main job is to get the essential information from the clients to verify the cause of the setbacks and report them. A help desk coordinator's job is to also encode the information into the tracking system. They will respond to the customer's queries. The coordinators should also be trainable. Answering customer's inquires is a tough job. In this task, you will meet cranky people who just lost money on a credit card. Some customers loose their temper. That is why it is very important for help desk coordinators to know how to handle these situations.

How your business can benefit from help desk: The help desk coordinator is an important part of any service-oriented business. Credit cards, airlines, communications are just some of the long list of businesses that need to train and hire them. Corporations should know that problems can occur in their business. That is why they have to be prepared from any setback in the industry. Preparing contingency plans and training helpdesk coordinators can save you from trouble. In fact, by designating help desk coordinators, you can have direct contact and feedback with your clients regarding your product. Through this, you will know the flaws and limitations of your merchandise. By logging in the client's inquiries, you can identify the problems and give solutions to it. In dealing with a service-oriented business, you have to know the problems that can take place and provide the necessary support to your clients. These help desk coordinators can facilitate inquiries, troubleshoot, and handle important information to aid your company, and satisfy customers.

Helpdesk: You Are a Specialist in Customer Support

All companies want to keep their customers loyal and satisfied. All businesses know that keeping a customer is less costly than finding a new one. That is why having a good relationship with their customers is very important to them. A helpdesk customer support specialist, whether in-house or outsourced, can mean a lot when it comes to after sales satisfaction.

The helpdesk customer support specialist is the front-liner of the company. He is responsible for directly facing and contacting the customer for after sales support, and other inquiries by the customer. A good helpdesk customer support specialist will be able to properly assist the customer in whatever inquiries and difficulties the customer may be facing. Aside from that, he should also be responsible for gathering and storing data about the customer so that it can be analyzed later for future potential sales and other purposes.

Being a helpdesk customer support specialist, he should be able to manage the company's professional relationship with the customer by providing support and assistance whether through the phone, e-mail or the Internet. This could include a direct interaction with the customer (phone, live chat, instant messaging, etc.) to resolve issues related to the product or service that was purchased. The company's objective is always to provide the best customer service support to its clients. It is the helpdesk customer support specialist's job to help the company attain its objective by responding to customer requests for assistance and support as soon as possible, and immediately document the report for future reference.

It is essential, therefore, that the helpdesk customer support specialist have excellent and professional communication skills, with customer service as his primary focus. He is a key factor in retaining customer loyalty and satisfaction; therefore, he should always strive to assist the customer in every way he can.

Being a Helpdesk Supervisor

All companies want to properly manage their relationships with customers to keep them loyal to their product or service. Whether it's storing or gathering data, customer support or after sales service, properly managing helpdesks is very important. A team of CRMs will naturally need a supervisor to properly handle them. A good helpdesk supervisor can assist the management in a number of ways. He is a trainer and an administrative officer, and also responsible for the smooth operation of his CRM team.

Helpdesk supervisors help in training, mentoring and coaching team members. A good helpdesk supervisor is able to select and train his agents, and keep them updated on the different processes and systems of customer relationship management. A clear understanding of the operational procedures of call centers is a requirement for every helpdesk supervisor, so he can manage his team's speed, work accuracy and prioritization, among other things. A helpdesk supervisor is there whenever there are questions his team needs assistance with. He should be available if there are difficult cases that need to escalate to the next level of help.

Of course, there are goals and targets that need to be achieved in every team. A helpdesk supervisor will always strive to achieve the targets in terms of turn around times, quality of service, response times, and customer satisfaction.

Whatever the CRM may be, helpdesk supervisors need to be on top of things by regularly submitting reports and keeping management informed of any developments or issues within his team and the company. A helpdesk supervisor should be able to evaluate and offer feedback on good performance, as well as those that need improvement. He should have a close professional relationship with his team in, and he must be able to inspire his team to work in an atmosphere of camaraderie and professionalism.

What is the Relationship Between the Help Desk, Support Specialist, Technical Support Specialist and Other IT Personnel?

Advances in Information Technology (IT) have made support systems necessary so that organizations, their customers, and even end users can cope when problems that arise from using IT systems. The software and hardware have intricate and sensitive technical components, which make it necessary for support systems to have competencies in managing these components. There are three specific areas of support:

The Help Desk: people who man the Help Desk are called the frontliners. They are the first people you talk to when you call up the help desk hotlines. As a rule, every call must be considered important and requiring swift action. The Help Desk not only answers calls, their staff must also attend to walk-ins, troubleshoot hardware and software problems at the drop of a hat, and monitor the status of pending cases. When the help desk has been able to identify the problem, troubleshoot it, and the case has been dealt with properly, then it is considered accomplished.

The Support Specialist: This team is those people equipped with more specialized information technology training. They act as a higher level of support for the Help Desk. The Support Specialist assists the Help Desk staff in troubleshooting PC and network problems; isolate and diagnose network problems; and monitor, test and document network infrastructure. Because of their more advanced training, the Help Desk refers hard to solve cases to them.

The Technical Support Specialist: This team is composed of employees who have the highest level of technical expertise in troubleshooting, problem resolution, and systems maintenance. When compared to an army, they are the elite forces (perhaps the

SWAT team of IT, if you will). This team must be equipped with specialized technical knowledge because they deal with extremely complicated cases. They are there to support the Help Desk and the Support Specialist in a cooperative manner, since these three groups are expected to work hand in hand to meet a common goal - solve every computer-related problem presented to them.

As far as other IT personnel are concerned, the three groups previously mentioned must be able to work with them as well. Everyone in the organization should be aware of the value of teamwork so that the organization will function like a well-oiled machine.

The Role of the IT Help Desk Clerk

Someone has to attend to your customers' complaints or needs. There are various complaints that your company receives every day, and these have to be diagnosed as to the degree of severity of the problem. To do this, you assign an initial contact, or an IT help desk clerk, to attend to the numerous calls and emails that your company is receiving on a day-to-day basis.

Roles of an IT help desk clerk are:

1. They must be able to resolve the problems submitted by clients immediately.
2. On IT related questions, the IT help desk clerk must have a basic knowledge of the software or application systems, to be able to give basic answers to basic questions as posed by the clients.
3. Problem reports need to be recorded or logged to track recurring problems, and find solutions to avoid future occurrences.
4. Try to resolve incidents based on personal expertise or experience. A colleague at work may be consulted, if in doubt, or if further clarification is needed.
5. To refer specialized or problems or lengthy inquiries to an "off-duty" help desk staff member. This is to provide unlimited or uninterrupted assistance should lengthy discussion be needed.
6. If the IT help desk clerk is not able to solve the problem or questions, the matter should be forwarded to the next level of support so the client doesn't have to wait.

The IT help desk clerk can be referred to as the front desk officer, and is highly regarded as an important asset in the company. They serve as front liners in receiving calls from clients, and therefore good communications skills and well-mannered individuals should be put in placed.

What IT Help Desk Software Covers?

Tracking down support requests and answering numerous emails can be a tedious job for the company. Whether an organization is small, medium or large, keeping track of support requests and numerous inquiries through emails can be a critical problem in managing your customer's needs.

If not equipped with the right tools, you will lose your customers as they begin to feel dissatisfaction with the service you provide. There is a need to equip your organization with an IT Help Desk Software. The IT help desk software provides your organization with the following benefits:

1. It allows the organization to have their help desk portal customized specific to employee-based needs;
2. It enables prioritization and managing the work orders centrally. With the IT help desk software, a trouble ticket system is provided;
3. It allows the tracking of assets and managing purchasing and receiving;
4. It improves the help desk process by means of the on-demand surveys and reports;
5. It allows a secure access to any web browser or location.

All that is required for IT help desk software is for users to have an Internet connection to serve their clients, anywhere and anytime. The software can be installed in any web server i.e. Linux, UNIX, NT, 2000, 2003, and XP Pro web servers. You can also select from five different databases such as flat file, MySQL, Microsoft SQL, Oracle, and PosgreSQL.

The IT desk help software is the solution you need in your organization to ensure that your firm communicates effectively within departments, and that you respond to your client's needs;

making sure that tracking and reporting issues are organized and prioritized. Keeping customers happy and getting relieved from the tedious hassle of tracking request support concerns; that is the power of this software.

Delivering Solutions Through Microsoft Helpdesk Remote Assistance

The most common method of support system for a help desk is via phone conversation between a customer and a technician. Where a customer describes the problem to the technician, and the latter tries to explain solution over the phone. This situation was found to be difficult to address both issues, and to be costly on the part of both of the calling parties. Microsoft Help Desk found a better way to efficiently hold problems and solutions on the support desk, through a built-in feature within the Microsoft Windows XP Professional. This built-in feature is known as Remote Assistance.

The Microsoft Help Desk Remote Assistance allows an employee to give permission to a technician, an administrator, or a similar expert to take a look into or control the employee's computer. The employee sets a limited time period for this. Remote Assistance includes computer control, text chat, voice chat, and file sharing; everything in one simple user friendly interface. The Microsoft Help Desk Remote Assistance resolves the problems addressed to technicians, without the technician having to sit down beside a complaining employee. The chat options are available for them to discuss the issues and they need not be connected through the phone to discuss it verbally. Discussions are also documented, rather than said verbally, which allows the employee to trace back whatever was missing during the chat discussion.

With the Microsoft Helpdesk Remote Assistance, you can make your clients satisfied as you delivered solutions remotely over the phone or online, and reduce cost as well.

The Work of a Network Administrator WAN Cisco Help Desk Analyst

Computer systems need proper administration and maintenance. There should be a focal person in charge to handle administrative support on all the software users within the work environment. An organization needs a network administrator who will design, install and support the local-area network (LAN), wide-area network (WAN), network segment, Internet, or intranet system. If you are a network administrator for a wide area network (WAN), you are required to maintain the hardware and software of the network, analyze problems, and monitor the network to see that the system is available for users. They also try to gather information to identify the needs of the customers and make use of this information to identify, interpret, and evaluate system and network requirements. Network WAN administrators may plan, coordinate, and implement network security measures.

A leading manufacturer of networking and inter-networking products is Cisco. Today it is highly desirable to have knowledge in Cisco technology. To be eligible for a Cisco certification you take an examination. A network administrator WAN Cisco help desk analyst will be responsible for the efficient use of the organization's network. The network administrator WAN Cisco help desk analyst will ensure that the computer site, as design for the organization and its components, are installed and working properly. Components referred to are: computers, the network, and software. Being part of the help desk, the network administrator WAN Cisco should monitor and make continuous adjustments, based on the network's current performance, and survey future network needs.

The network administrator WAN Cisco help desk analyst is involved in troubleshooting problems as reported by users. They make use of automated network monitoring systems and recommend enhancements in the implementation of future servers and networks.

Why Network Administrators and Technical Support Help Desk are Important to Your Company

Companies these days have IT departments that help business work. Your business needs to have a secured system that will support your company. In this way, you will be able to work faster and more efficiently.

Network administrators design, support and install Internet, network segments, and applications needed in your organization. They support and give solutions for software used every day in offices, small and medium businesses, large corporations and, of course, the government. One of the major responsibilities of a network administrator is to see to it that they maintain the system and networking of the company. They also analyze the problems and check regularly the users' accessibility. This group of people collects the necessary data to know the client's needs. They use this data and information to figure out and assess possible improvements to the system. They also set up a plan to organize and apply a security system.

Service oriented firms need to have technical support help desks to answer queries from their customers. Basically, computer users have a hard time troubleshooting, especially with Internet connections. The job of the technical support help desk is to resolve problems like this. Printer, keyboards, monitors, hardware / software problems, and installations processes are just some of the key responsibilities of this job. The help desk for technical support should train and equip the users with the necessary practical knowledge in computers. This help desk should also supervise the performance of the system and if it works properly. They should also evaluate programs created, as to how they are used, and their efficacy to the company. They principally help customers find solutions to their computer problems.

Network administrators and technical support help desk are a crucial part of today's business settings. These two units basically help the company to effectively support the system in communication. Without them, it is impossible to communicate.

The Basics About the Online Help Desk

When IT customers required precise information, data and documents (especially if they are new end users), network service providers came up with the so-called Online Help Desk (OHD) system. This system is used to cater to the demands of, and answer questions of, clients; and resolve problems they may encounter, such as error codes. The OHD was designed for a specific user group, which is why it maintains a distinct set of performance objectives and has a clear-cut purpose. The Performance Support System (PSS), also called the OHD, was made so that actual usage by most system users would match the ideal optimal system usage expected.

The OHD encompasses very useful elements, such as databases, tools, and documentation; so that new users can deal with information access needs, and other production-oriented goals. To clarify further what the performance support system is about, it is not meant for training; rather, it is an aid to improve performance. The customer is guided through the support services he can expect, based on the current support and maintenance agreement provided.

Due to the high level of demand for Internet-based information access in the market, the small size of the market cannot guarantee the effective and efficient use of resources.

The emphasis of a PSS is on understanding cognitive tools rather than training. It is up to the utility to choose which user-related information can contribute toward understanding by the technical support staff of the resources provided to them. There is a relationship between OHD and instruments known as prosthetic tools, which are geared for use by the UCD community in the area. Such tools help the online desk to use the make page utility that the new users rely on to create home pages.

Help Desk Receptionist: More than Just a Clerical Job

These days, being a help desk receptionist is an in demand job all over the world. Companies have enormously improved on customer service and handling queries. If you want a career as a receptionist, and are looking for a help desk job today, then check this out!

What are the responsibilities?

Being a help desk receptionist is a multi-tasking job. Some might think that it is just one of those easy clerical jobs. Being in customer service is a tough job. It requires an attentive mind with knowledge on applications used in the help desk. This job may seem easy with its job title, but being a help desk receptionist means meeting and talking to people. Phone call inquires, scheduling, arranging conference meetings, and data entry jobs are commonly included in their job description. And, since the receptionist is the first person to be seen in a company, help desk receptionists should be presentable. In some companies, they require particular height and physical requirement.

Computer literacy is equally important. Computer skills are needed to finish tasks like spreadsheets; Windows or Mac knowledge is a significant factor in considering an applicant. Call center abilities and being fluent in the required language is substantially important. In order to answer customer queries, you have to speak fluently and know how to respond to them. Basically, when you deal with customers, you have to work fast. Inbound calls can give receptionists a hard time. They have to be familiar with the applications and systems that will aid them in answering the questions. This includes product information, delivery confirmations, complaints, billing confirmations, promos and many more.

A help desk receptionist is a clerical job that requires a systematic and organized candidate. It is like managing a company's clients, and meeting the requirements of managers. This is a challenging yet exciting multi-tasking job. Being a help desk receptionist will help you meet new faces and exercise your people skills.

Benefits of Software Help Desk

Customers are your number priority in the operation of your business. As your company receives complaints and inquiries via phone or email, these issues need to be attended to immediately. A company needs to find solutions and get in touch with their customers as soon as possible, so as not for the latter to feel dissatisfied with the company's service.

Software Help Desk is a support solution. The software seeks to provide a ticket tracking system that keeps track of incidents reported by customers to the company's support departments.

The foregoing are the benefits derived by users from the use of software help desk:

1. Customer Benefits. Customers are given fully featured access to the support portal, which allows them to submit their support requests, or make use of search articles or frequently asked questions. From this portal, customers can track the action taken by the company on their request and respond to them.
2. Staff Benefit. The software help desk allows staff to look over the outstanding requests that have been assigned to them, or to their department. Permissions on the access to other departments may be limited. Since support requests carry a track number, staff assignments are identified as to their status and priority.
3. Management Benefit. The software help desk provides a management report that covers the number of requests received, the department that took action or respond to the support requests. It permits management to have a real time overview of how effective staff communicates with customers.

Software help desk is the solution to keep your customer, staff and management on top of the situation.

The Benefits Derived From Teaching Help Desk Staff

If you have gone as far up the help desk department ladder in your organization as you can possibly go (without becoming the owner of the company or enterprise, that is), what is the next possible step in your career? Earning more money? Perhaps. Or maybe you would want to consider a new stage in your career, teaching help desk staff the ropes of working in the help desk department?

Why would anyone want to resort to teaching help desk staff as a new career option? There are many reasons; again, some people do it because they are able to earn more from this position. But still, others agree to teach help desk personnel because they feel a need to pass on to the next generation what they have learned from all their years of working in the help desk department.

What can be learned from old-timers like you, in a field like Information Technology where knowledge from just a few years ago easily becomes obsolete and unusable due to the adoption of newer and more high-tech systems? To start off, you can teach help desk agents how to handle angry, frustrated callers with professionalism, finesse, and poise. That kind of skill never goes out of style. You can also show the next generation what old systems have in common with the newer and more advanced ones. Yes, every system that has come along has some basic knowledge that was developed in the past. So, even though you may not be as knowledgeable about some of these new systems, it is still possible for you to propose solutions that worked in the past in similar systems.

Can teaching help desk staff ever become passé? Not very likely. As long as there is an influx of new people into the IT world, there will always be a need for people patient enough to train them.

Let the Help Desk Support Consultant / Analyst do the Work

The computer has been an integral part of our everyday living, as it is found to be useful in our home, workplace and at schools. The hardware and software of computers are man-made. These parts are subject to wear and tear, and prone to breakdown. Whether it is malfunction or improper use of the operational features, these situations need to be addressed and answered.

Due to the various types of computer problems addressed every day; there is a high demand for help desk support consultants / analysts. The help desk support consultant/analyst provides technical assistance, support, and advice to customers and other users. They are the troubleshooters within the help desk support. They interpret the problems addressed by customers, and provide technical support for hardware, software, and systems used. They are in charge of answering the phone calls of customers, and use automated diagnostic programs to analyze problems, thereby preventing recurrence of the same issue in the future. A help desk support consultant / analyst may either work for a company that sells computers, or be directly employed by hardware and software vendors. Some work for help-desk or support service firms on a contractual basis. They work on monitors, keyboards, printers, and mice; they install, modify, clean, and repair computer hardware and software. Help desk support consultants / analysts are sometimes tasked to write manuals and train new computer users in the use of hardware and software. They are in charge of overseeing the daily performance of the company's computer systems, as well as the evaluation of the software programs as to their usefulness.

Among everything else, your client's satisfaction is your first priority. Let the help desk support consultant / analyst resolve the problem addressed by your clients immediately on the first level.

The Web Based Help Desk Software for you

As your customers demand more, you need to give priority to attaining your customers' satisfaction. You should realize that your customers deserve great service. Losing your customers would mean great loss of the hard-earned money you have placed on your business, as well as gaining potential customers.

Software made available to answer your organization's, as well as your customers' needs on a 24/7 basis, is known as Web Based Help Desk Software. The web based help desk software is installed on your web server. It improves your communication with your customers, and keeps things within your company organized and efficient. With the web-based help desk software, your technicians or customers don't need to have the software on their computers to use it, in as much as it is 100% web browser based. The software enables your customer to search for things they need answers to immediately, without waiting for the following day to call your company. Where help support complaints before were made through phone calls or mailed through regular or email; the web-based help desk software is the solution to provide your customers ultimate service. During the support request or when the complaint is addressed, customers are notified via email with the actions undertaken by your company. Customers can log in and check the request support status or make an update. They can also work hand in hand with the technician in charge of the support request.

The web based help desk software also seeks to replace your support email link. It's time to say goodbye to those messy emails that fill your inbox, and those support requests that you fail to crack down on. Give your customers the ultimate satisfaction they deserve and make them happy.